Having The Talk: The Four Keys to Your Parents' Safe Retirement

By Jack Tatar

16 15 14 13   10 9 8 7 6 5 4 3 2 1

Having The Talk: The Four Keys to Your Parents' Safe Retirement
ISBN-10: 0985082046
ISBN-13: 978-0-9850820-4-8

Copyright © 2013 by Jack Tatar
Pennington, NJ 08534
Library of Congress Control Number: 2013900756

Published by PeopleTested® Publications
www.PeopleTested.com

Printed in the United States of America. All rights reserved under International Copyright Law. Contents and/or cover may not be reproduced in whole or in part in any form without the express written consent of the Publisher.

Table of Contents

Introduction 9

Section One:
Having the Talk with Your Parents About Retirement 15

    Chapter 1   Why Have the Talk? 21

    Chapter 2   When Do I Have the Talk? 27

    Chapter 3   What's Covered in the Talk? 31

    Chapter 4   How Do I Have the Talk? 39

Section Two: Financial Preparedness and the Talk 47

    Chapter 5   The Retirement Backdrop 49

    Chapter 6   Working with a Professional 51

    Chapter 7   Pieces of the Retirement Planning Pie 55

    Chapter 8   The Financial Plan 63

    Chapter 9   Long Term Care 71

    Chapter 10   Moving From the Family Home 77

    Chapter 11   Government Help 81

Section Three: Physical Health and the Talk 87

    Chapter 12   The Incredible Cost-Saving Benefits
                             of a Walk in the Park 89

    Chapter 13   Having the Health Talk 93

    Chapter 14   Exercise: Living Healthier Step-by-Step 99

    Chapter 15   Eating Your Way to Good Health 107

Chapter 16	Your Brain as the Key to Longevity	121
Chapter 17	Your Medical Team	127
Chapter 18	For Caregivers	133

Section Four: Mental Attitude and the Talk 139

Chapter 19	Attitude is Everything	141
Chapter 20	Transitioning Into Retirement	149
Chapter 21	Leaving a Legacy	155
Chapter 22	Gaining Peace of Mind	165
Chapter 23	The Joys of Friends	171
Chapter 24	The Importance of Beliefs	177

Section Five: Staying Involved and the Talk 187

Chapter 25	The Secret Ingredient to Longevity	189
Chapter 26	Begin at Home	193
Chapter 27	Places to Play	199
Chapter 28	Sails Ahoy	203
Chapter 29	Getting the Most Out of Working in Retirement	211
Chapter 30	Volunteering	219
Chapter 31	The Magic of Social Media	225

Peace of Mind 233

About the Author 237

To my Maudee Ann,

the light of my life.

Thanks

As I've learned in the past, writing a book is a team effort. This book would not have been possible without the help of the best friends and partners a guy could have.

First of all, to my wonderful wife, Maude who had the idea for this book. Thanks for always keeping me focused on how I can create things that help others. To my terrific children, Eric and Grace of whom I am so proud and grateful to God for having brought into my life. I love you all!

No book on this subject is possible without thanking my dear friend, Sam Kirk.

Once again, any reason for this book's readability is due to my good friend and editor, the great Ira-Neil Dittersdorf. This Bloomsday is on me, buddy!

Heartfelt thanks must go out to the magnificent Karen Lacey for once again, all of your help and skills to make this book possible.

I'd also like to thank my publishing team of Lisa DeSpain and Steven Peterson for their great work and assistance in making this book a reality.

I'm fortunate to be part of the Marketwatch.com group of The Retire-Mentors and I'd especially like to thank my good friend, and leading retirement writer, Bob Powell for all of his support and assistance.

I'd also like to thank my sister-in-law, Margaret Anderson for being the first success story of my books. May your retirement continue to be safe and long! You're an inspiration to many who hope to thrive in retirement as you are doing.

To my sister, Regina for all of your help, expertise and friendship. It's always great to have a Director of Nursing a phone call away. And to my terrific niece and nephew, Jillian and Sean.

Of course, thanks always go to my mom and dad, Bob and Ellen Tatar, who I think of every day and continue to be my inspiration to help others.

Last but not least, I'd like to thank all of those readers who wrote me such wonderful notes and kind words about my books and articles over the last few years. Your words keep me going and believing that maybe these little books can make a difference. Thanks (and keep writing!).

Introduction

"Don't collect things."

If you have parents who are in their advanced stages of life, you are aware of the many challenges that exist for them. You may even have become acutely aware of how these challenges also impact you.

Caregiving for a parent or another elderly family member can make your already harried life even more difficult.

Maybe you've had a frustrating chat with a parent that covered the gamut from their burial wishes to how they should get someone to clean their house.

It seems that ultimately we all end up having a conversation with our parents about such things as their financial estate, end-of-life considerations, and living arrangements. The problem is quite often that we have these conversations too late. For instance, we have them in times of crisis or when there is little that we can do to change or soften the impact of these decisions. We end up having discussions about living arrangements when such arrangements need to be made right away and when they might incur significant financial damage. Or we have discussions about moving money into trusts when a parent is hospitalized, only to realize that a "look back" provision will significantly hinder these plans.

Let's not forget those situations that occur after a sibling or family member had an "expectation" that they would receive mom's valuable artwork or dad's old pipe collection, only to find that other plans were made. This "unspoken agreement" results in a lengthy time of "not speaking" among family members.

The reality is that there are many things that need to be considered with an aging parent.

In much the same manner as your parents presented "the talk" to you as children and young adults around topics such as sex, drugs, and life, there's a time (and a responsibility) for you to have a talk with them around the topics that are vital to them in their later stages of life.

Just as the talk that they gave you took many shapes and forms, so will this talk. It may not be the "Hallmark" version with everyone sitting around the dining room table (but it might be). It might be a talk that occurs in pieces over time, perhaps in the car or on multiple visits. The talk will occur in many different ways for different people.

The point is to do it and do it early.

That's why you should position your talk about retirement as close to the onset of your parents' retirement as possible. This will help ensure that everyone is speaking with their fullest mental capacities and you don't suffer through your parents' retirement with you or your siblings having unspoken expectations and impressions of what will happen.

When you have the talk about retirement, you can discuss many positive things that your parents will encounter in the next phase of their life, which may be the most fun one of their lives. It provides you a time to celebrate the accomplishment of their retirement and speak positively about all of the wonderful things that will happen for your parents.

Above all, have a talk that is positive and expansive and focuses on the realistic aspects that this later stage of life will bring.

As I had mentioned, you may not be able to discuss everything that needs to be discussed in a single sitting, but by having it early and in a positive light, you set the stage for continued discussions that will allow you to cover all of the areas you need to.

By putting it in the context of retirement, it will also allow you to incorporate my strategy of the "Four Keys," which I believe will lead to a safer and longer retirement for your parents.

The Four Keys strategy provides the tools to not only view retirement just as a financial decision, but also to evaluate the following as keys to ensuring a safe retirement:

- Financial Preparedness
- Health & Wellness
- Mental Attitude
- Staying Involved

As I stated in my previous book, *Safe 4 Retirement: The Four Keys to a Safe Retirement*, "Most books about retirement written today deal exclusively about financial planning for retirement. My intent with this book is to present a holistic approach to retirement planning and living in retirement, more than what you'll find in most other books about retirement."[1]

The book that you are holding was written to help the adult child to address these areas of concern for them and their parents. The intent of this book is twofold:

- First, to give you an overview of what are the areas of concern that an adult child should be aware of for his or her aging parents. I'll cover not just the financial matters of concern, but also health matters, both physically and mental, and the need to create, nurture, and maintain a social structure for our parents. And, we'll explore all these topics in a holistic manner.

- Second, my goal is to provide you with a mechanism and resource that will allow you to have these conversations at an appropriate and earlier stage so that proper planning can take place to allow your parents to enjoy this phase of their lives.

We'll explore each of the Four Keys extensively in this book in order that you are armed with enough information on each of them. You can then use those aspects of each key that are most appropriate for you to cover during your talk with your parents.

---

1 *Safe 4 Retirement: The Four Keys to a Safe Retirement*, People Tested Publications, 2011

By expanding the retirement discussion beyond just financial matters, you'll be exploring the elements of your parents' lives that will help them live a longer and happier retirement. You'll also ensure yourself that you're covering all of the topics that you should to help both your parents and yourself plan for this next phase of their lives.

The best laid financial plans for retirement can be severely impacted by health issues of not only your retired parents but also by those of other family members. You will also find that your parents will encounter tragedies such as the loss of friends and family members. How they deal with these matters and how strong a social structure they have will impact their ability to address these challenges.

For these and so many others reasons, you owe it to your parents and yourself to have a holistic discussion of retirement, rather than just one that covers financial matters. The Four Keys approach will help you to do that.

Although I'll provide you with some good mechanisms for having the talk, the reality is that you'll have to do what feels right and most appropriate for your own situation.

As anyone who has read my previous book is aware, this topic has been a very personal one for me. I wrote that book as a way to deal with the loss of both of my parents within six months of each other.

In order to understand this tragedy, I researched and learned that the "broken heart" syndrome is a real one. It is true that many retired and elderly spouses will die within a short period of time of each other. What is also true is that the most resilient spouses are those who have a strong social structure and are able to maintain a positive attitude toward life. [2]

Obviously, this can be difficult at a time of tragedy, but what I learned and built into the Four Keys is that there's a need to address these nonfinancial topics as a way to allow seniors and the retired to live a longer and safer life.

When my parents announced their retirement to me, I was thrilled and happy for them. The only thing I said to them at that time was to my mom, "Don't collect things."

---

[2] http://safe4retirement.com/is-it-common-for-a-spouse-to-die-so-soon-after-the-loss-of-the-other-spouse

As I went through the tragedy of losing my parents and having many discussions with them at a time that ultimately proved to be too late, I realized that I should've said so many other things at that time rather than just voice my concern that my mom would collect spoons or ugly dolls in her spare time.

I've been heartened by the responses I've received by the many who have read my books and have told me that they appreciate the more holistic view of retirement planning. The stories that I've heard by both retirees and the children of retirees have proven to me that lessons can be learned by the darkest tragedies that can ultimately help others.

This book is written for all of those adult children who will have the strength to have the talk with their parents about retirement. Just as your parents nervously had the talk with you about important matters, after they had them, they were satisfied that they were not only doing something that was required of them as parents but was something that they did out of their love for you.

Now it's your chance.

May this book provide you with the tools and resources to have the talk.

You supply the courage and the love.

Section One

Having the Talk with Your Parents About Retirement

Each year, concerns mount about the ability for Americans to retire safely. Only 14% of Americans feel comfortable that they can retire.³ In terms of money for retirement, 42% fear they might outlive their savings.⁴ The sad fact is that 57% of pre-retirees haven't even created a concrete retirement plan.⁵

When you add in the concerns about the rising costs of healthcare, the reality is that 63% of baby boomers (those born between 1946 and 1964) lack the confidence that they will have enough money for medical expenses once they retire. It becomes an even more serious concern when you realize that 70% of people over age 65 will require some form of long-term care.⁶

The plain truth is that every single one of us is going to age and will probably need help looking after ourselves at some point in time. The alternative, an early death, isn't that attractive. It's undeniable that as we live longer, our bodies, minds, and abilities wear down. Sometimes this happens gradually; sometimes it occurs instantly through a catastrophic event, like the sudden onset of an illness or an accident.

Clearly, these are concerns for those entering retirement; however, they should also be the concerns of those considering retirement at some point in the future. Adult children who are interested in helping their retiring, or retired, parents to live happily and safely in their retirements also need to be aware of these issues.

Given the inevitability of our aging process and the concerns that people have about thriving and living safely in retirement, a recent American As-

---

3 According to a survey by the Employee Benefit Research Institute, only 14% of workers feel "very confident" they will have enough money to live comfortably in retirement, 38% of workers say they are "somewhat confident," and 23% say they are "not at all confident." The results have remained relatively unchanged since hitting an all-time low in 2009.
http://money.cnn.com/2012/03/13/retirement/workers-confidence/index.htm
4 Cogent Research 2010
5 Healthcare Expenses and Retirement Income, Insured Retirement Institute, January 2011
6 U.S. Department of Health and Human Services, National Clearinghouse for Long Term Care Information, October 22, 2008.

sociation of Retired Persons (AARP) survey found that two-thirds of adult children have never talked about these matters with their parents.[7]

So how can it be that these vital aging and end-of-life conversations are never undertaken or done too late at best?

Is it because they're just plain awkward for most people?

Is it because we never know when the time is right to have them?

Is it because we're afraid of what our parents will think our motives are for having this discussion?

It's hard enough to imagine our parents as senior citizens. The leap from authoritative provider to a frail and sometimes confused elderly person seems too great. Trust me, it's hard for them to stomach this, too, and they're fully aware of it.

So the thought of sitting down with your parents or older relative or friend and discussing personal financial and health related information is right up there in attractiveness with being audited by the IRS.

Now, let's not paint a dire picture of retirement. The reality is that retirement can, and often is, the best phase of a person's life. It's the time he or she has worked hard for and has dreamed of. It's a time to enjoy the stage of life when you're in control and can benefit from the fruits of your labor. Retirement comes with great trips, quality time with the grandkids, and activities with friends where there's no need to watch the clock.

As the children of retiring parents, it should be rewarding to watch our parents enter this new phase of their lives. It's a time to celebrate their labors and efforts. It's a time in which we can help our parents achieve what they've always dreamed of doing in much the same way they helped us to achieve our dreams.

It's also a time to recognize that along with new-found freedoms, retirement brings the need to consider many issues in order to ensure a long and safe retirement for our parents. You hope your aging parents, relatives, and friends will always be healthy and mentally sharp. It's easier to see them that

---

[7] http://www.rureadyca.org/sites/default/files/uploads/TheConversation.pdf

way. But it's not realistic, and in the long run avoiding these matters is not what's best for them.

As the adult child of a retiring or retired parent, you may hold the key to ensuring that your parents enjoy a safe retirement. In order to achieve this, you will need to be an active participant in the discussion, planning, and implementation phase of your parents' retirement.

The reality is that you will eventually have The Talk with your parents about retirement. Unfortunately, it often happens when a parent is in crisis mode brought on by poor health, the death of a loved one, or a significant change in their financial situation. Sometimes it's caused by something in your own life or that of one of your siblings. Many times the talk comes about when caregiving is required. Unfortunately, at this point you might be dealing with a situation where the mental capacities of a parent are significantly impaired and you're left wondering if you're doing the right thing.

It's my goal in this book for you to have the talk sooner rather than later. Having it earlier will ensure that you are dealing with parents at their fullest mental capacities. As well, they may be dealing with children who have expectations that can cause major family differences if they aren't dealt with early on.

In this book you will be guided through the process and details for how to bring up these conversations and what to cover. I'm writing this book for the adult children of retirees, but it can also be read by retirees or pre-retirees who will see the value in having the talk early and can be proactive in getting the family together sooner rather than later. Either way, the goal is to provide a book that family members can read so they all benefit from the concepts and ideas. In fact, sitting down together with this book and its action plan and checklists may be a great way to ensure success in having this discussion.

In this section I'll cover four areas:

- Why Have the Talk?
- When Do I Have the Talk?

- What Is Covered in the Talk?
- How Do I Have the Talk?

In the remaining sections I'll cover in detail what you and/or your parents can do to get the most out of retirement. I've broken this down into four key areas of well-being: financial preparedness, health and wellness, mental attitude, and staying involved. This follows the tenets of my strategy for a safe retirement as outlined in my book *Safe 4 Retirement: The Four Keys to a Safe Retirement*.[8]

Sitting down and discussing these matters isn't rocket science. Although many of the subjects I'll go into will seem like common sense, others may seem contrary to what we were raised to believe. Each, however, is backed up with both scientific proof and real-life stories from people who are putting the truth in the phrase "the Golden Years."

The goal is to equip you with tools, resources, and tips to make this a positive experience for all. This book will not only help you and your parents, but can serve to bring you together closer as a family. And believe me, it will make your parents happy.

---

[8] http://www.Safe4Retirement.com

1

Why Have the Talk?

What is this all-important talk and why should we have it?

Put yourself in the scenario a friend of mine experienced. His mother, let's call her Judith, lived on her own in a high-rise apartment building in a medium-sized city. For years she fared well and lived a healthy, active life. The son, we'll call him Richard, also had a busy life raising his family and blazing a trail in his executive career.

But life changes, and it certainly did for Judith. Her health gradually failed. Not in dramatic leaps that would have alerted her son, but she just slowed down. She started missing bill payments and doctor's appointments. Her driving deteriorated, but fortunately she never caused an accident.

Until one day when she collapsed on her living room floor with a stroke. Hours passed before anyone found her, and so instead of receiving critical treatment in the early phases of the disease, she lay helpless as it took its full toll.

Judith survived, but she was not nearly in the same state as she was before. Richard had to take over all of her financial, health, and lifestyle decisions. Typical of children and their post-World War II era parents, Richard had never discussed financial matters with his mother. He had no idea what accounts and investments she had, and he certainly didn't know any of the passwords she used to access her financial information.

They'd never discussed what her wishes were if a catastrophe like this should occur. Richard could communicate with his mother, but the stroke had left her befuddled and unable to speak clearly. Where would she live? Who would look after her? How would he make sure she was as comfortable and happy as possible? Did she have long-term care insurance or would this drain her finances and possibly sap some of his?

Having the talk before it's needed is like having car insurance before you get in an accident. You can't rush out and buy the insurance to pay for things after you've just totaled your car.

By clearly discussing financial, health, and lifestyle issues before the information is needed, much of the turmoil and concern experienced in Richard's and his mother's situation could have been avoided.

Let's take a look at another real-life situation. Two parents have worked hard their entire lives. They divided up their two careers so that at least one parent was home with their children at all times during the day. The husband worked during the day as a civil worker and even after retirement continued to work for another 20 years in jobs ranging from a gas station attendant to cleaning toilets at hospitals in order to make ends meet.

The wife worked for over 35 years as an overnight nurse at a hospital emergency room. When she retired, the thought of switching her sleeping habits around was a welcome concern for her.

Their adult children were thrilled when their parents announced that they would both finally hang up their spurs and retire. And retire they did. However, it was only when the husband became sick that these parents began to open up about their financial and health situations to their adult children.

This left little time for considering healthcare options due to estate lookback requirements and a lack of clarity about what each parent actually wanted should caregiving become a need. Fortunately, the financial situations were worked out during this time of crisis, but many other aspects of their retirement were left out of the discussion.

These considerations became a moot point when they each died within six months of each other. Many wondered if this was an example of the "broken heart" syndrome that many blame on the close deaths of retired spouses. The son of these parents was left with the nagging question of why didn't he have discussions sooner with his retired parents so that perhaps they could have enjoyed a longer and safer retirement?

I know this story well because I am that son. I didn't discuss their financial situation. I didn't discuss their health situation and the importance of taking care of their health in retirement. I didn't discuss the need to maintain a positive attitude and social interactions in retirement.

If I had, would they have lived longer in retirement? Well, the research around broken heart syndrome proves that a positive attitude and a strong social support structure help make a surviving spouse more resilient after the death of their husband or wife.[9]

The·talk is not only about money and finances. It's about all of those aspects that contribute toward ensuring that your parents enjoy a long and safe retirement.

So, if having the talk is so important, than why don't more people do it? As I mentioned previously, it's awkward discussing death and money with your parents. Equally for them, it's tough bringing these issues up with your children. Parents don't want to be a burden. They'll manage fine; I mean, they have up until now, right? However, these aren't the only reasons the talk is difficult.

To put it all into perspective, it helps to understand the different developmental stages we go through in life. Author David Solie summed this up well in his brilliant book *How to Say It to Seniors: Closing the Communication Gap with Our Elders*.[10] Rather than thinking of our elderly parents as "losing it" or taken to "rambling on about the same old stories," geriatric experts like Solie claim that the aging process is actually a developmental stage. This stage is rife with the potential for personal development and growth, even as society seems to push mature people more and more to the side.

---

9 http://safe4retirement.com/is-it-common-for-a-spouse-to-die-so-soon-after-the-loss-of-the-other-spouse
10 David Solie, *How to Say It to Seniors: Closing the Communication Gap with Our Elders*, (Upper Saddle River, NJ: Prentice Hall Press, 2004) David Solie.

By understanding these developmental stages and, therefore, why older people seem to act "differently," we can not only facilitate their growth, but also make inroads in coming to terms with our own aging process.

Solie mentions five developmental stages in his book and the conflicting dynamics inherent in each:

1) The terrible twos. This is the age when a child needs his mother, but yet is also developing his own personality and identity. As with all stages, the two psychological drivers are opposing each other.

2) The terrible teens. Remember them? Or maybe you have children living at home refreshing your memory. These years are filled with the same drivers and conflicts as those of the two year olds, they're just presented differently. The teen isn't ready to leave home yet, but is struggling with the need for independence.

3) The 20s or so. Here the drivers are flipped. You've moved out of your parent's home and independence has been achieved, but now there's a strong desire to share your life with someone and perhaps start your own family.

4) The 40s or so. This is where most of us are firing on all cylinders. We're established in our careers and our families. Sure, we'll have had upsets like divorces, job losses, and the like, but for the most part we have a handle on life and are making it all happen. Whether a CEO or a soccer mom, we're task driven, goal oriented, and busy checking items off our to-do lists. But we are also feeling the need to contribute to our communities. We work toward personal achievements, but we are also driven to give outwardly.

5) The 60s, 70s, and onward. Pivotal to the experience of aging is a sense of loss of control. Our minds and bodies do not function like they used to, and society seems to lose sight of our value. Therefore, a primary driver at this developmental stage is the need to hang on to what control we have left. In contrast to this is the need to go inward and make sense of the life we've lived. Solie calls this searching for

our legacy. As you will see, these two drivers not only conflict with each other, but they also conflict with those of the forty-year-olds.[11]

It's these very different motivations operating within adult children versus those in their parents that are causing part of the problem.

When an adult child says, "You've missed an electricity payment, I need to help you with paying your bills." The retiree might be hearing, "I'm going to take away one more bit of the control you're hanging on to so desperately."

When the child says, "This home isn't safe any longer. Let's go look at that assisted care living facility up the road." The retiree is thinking, "Not only won't I be able to live in my own home and make my own decisions, but now I can't even live amongst the memories that have made up my life." These are crucial issues for anyone over the age of seventy.

Adult children are working from their set of drivers, which include fast action and decision-making. The mature retiree is working from his or her set of drivers: hanging on to control first, and when this is accomplished, going inward to reflect on what their life has meant.

I'm going to walk you through how to deal with all of this. First, let's look into the next question:

---

11   David Solie, *How to Say It to Seniors: Closing the Communication Gap with Our Elders*, (Upper Saddle River, NJ: Prentice Hall Press, 2004) David Solie.

2

When Do I Have the Talk?

The best time to have the talk is well before you need it. Ideally, even before your parents have retired. This will allow for a richer and more intelligent conversation. As I wrote about extensively in my previous book, retiring successfully entails far more than just having a set number of dollars in your savings account.

Those people happiest in their retirement years have not just financial health, but stay physically fit and eat right, look after their mental acumen and attitude, and have close relationships with friends and family.

The talk I'm discussing in this book includes planning for health and success in each of those areas, too. As a retiree, you need to make sure your children know what you want and how you expect to live your life. As the adult child of a retiree, you can help facilitate the process of aging in the best way possible. An extra perk: When it comes your time to retire and address these same issues, you'll have already traveled down that road and will be able to apply your experience.

What you don't want is have the same thing happen that Richard and his mother, Judith, had happen. By the time they got around to the issues, the crisis had already happened. Richard ended up having to fumble through the dark trying to figure out what his mother's real wishes were.

I also hope that this book will help you avoid my own situation and my despair at leaving so many questions unasked of my parents as they entered retirement.

As I mentioned earlier, you will eventually have the talk with your parents, but often it happens too late. At that point you're operating in crisis mode, often with a parent with diminished mental capacities. You can also run into situations when more than one sibling is involved or even children from different marriages and unspoken expectations can exist. These are much better fleshed out and dealt with head on. The goal should be "the earlier the better."

Remember also that people age differently. Your neighbor Joe may be gray-haired and walk with a stoop at 70, while your own father at the same age may be preparing for his first triathlon. Partly it's genes, partly it's how we have lived and are currently living our lives. But mostly it's attitude.

So just waltzing in to have the talk with your father who's on his way out to the gym, after finishing a 20-mile bike ride, and before he leaves for the symposium he's giving later that evening, might not be the appropriate age specific time.

Use your judgment. But remember, crises can happen at any age. In this book, we'll help with openings or ice-breakers that can lead to having the talk.

If you're a retiree reading this who feels invincible and doesn't have the impending need to discuss these matters, remember that life can be fragile. I'm sure you can think of a friend or family member who has proven this to you.

To you I say, if your children haven't initiated the talk, reach out to them. You've always been a leader to them, and this may need to be another matter that you have to take the lead on. When you read through this book, you'll recognize the peace and comfort that having the talk will bring to all family members, regardless of who initiated it.

For the adult children of retirees or pre-retirees, if you haven't had the talk already and you're seeing signs of deteriorating mental or physical health, don't wait any longer. Understand that when signs of deterioration exist, they might affect the quality of your parents' decisions right now. In this case, you must act now.

Old age can be overwhelming. It's not just the physical changes—the creaky knees and aches and pains that predict rain better than any meteorologist—but also the mind slows down. We've all experienced it even if we're still in our roaring 40s. We even refer to them as "senior moments."

To a certain extent this is actually a healthy aspect of aging, because it allows the person to begin the reflection process that helps them figure out the meaning of their life. But when the slowing mind gets in the way of managing the financial, health, or safety aspects of living, this previously benevolent characteristic turns into a danger.

Stressful events can hasten the advance of aging. This could be due to the death of a spouse, the onset of a life threatening illness, or other shock to the normal routine of life.

Be on the lookout for red flags that signal all is not well. These could be in the form of:

- worsening health issues that are painful and/or effect mobility
- trouble with previously routine tasks such as balancing a checkbook
- an increase in forgetfulness such as missing bill payments
- cognitive impairment that goes beyond normal "senior moments"
- a decrease in personal hygiene
- trouble keeping the home clean and repaired
- a tendency toward depression and isolation

I recommend having the talk early as the best alternative overall. If your parents are zipping around as if they're 40, there may not seem to be a rush, but this might actually be the best time to have the talk. They're clear thinking, satisfied with life, and dreaming of their next phase. It may be the ideal time to sit down with them. If, on the other hand, they show signs of slowing, you shouldn't delay.

If you're a retiree or pre-retiree, leave your ego at the door and sit your children down to talk about the issues I outline in this book. Especially do so if you sense your having increased difficulty with life's daily issues. In the long and short run, it's the best thing for everyone.

So, now we know why to have the talk and when to have it. Let's now go into what you should actually be discussing.

3

What's Covered in the Talk?

Here my goal is to provide you with a snapshot of what to expect. This way you'll have a bird's eye view of the process. As you go forward, you can refer to the specific section that applies and the corresponding action plans and checklists.

In my previous book, I covered the Four Keys for a successful retirement life. My approach is holistic and, in many circles, untraditional. I believe, and have seen this with clients, family, and friends, that to be happily retired means looking after yourself and your loved ones in a robust and thoughtful way. It's not all about money. In fact, most retirees report that once they have enough money to retire, any additional funds don't significantly add to their happiness.

Happiness in retirement means you've got a handle on your finances, health, attitude, and are enjoying an active social life.

So for retirees, pre-retirees, and their children, going through the process of discussing each of these areas will pay off in happiness and well-being for years to come.

As you go through this book, we'll explore each of the Four Keys in more detail and provide in depth questions and topics for discussion. This will help to ensure that you and your parents feel comfortable that the talk will lead to a safe retirement.

I'll give you a general sense of what you should be discussing in each of the Four Keys.

Financial Health

The world is abound with financial planners and advisors who can be a key part of your financial planning process. As with any profession, some are good and some should be in another line of work?[12]

The level of trust between investors and those in the financial services industry has been dealt a major blow due to the recent financial crisis. A recent AP poll showed that 78% of Americans mistrust banks and lenders. In another, only 17% trust their financial provider.[13] With these numbers, how should you view the use of a financial advisor?

If your parents have a financial advisor they trust, that can be a very good thing; however, you may want to ensure that this advisor has your parents' best interests at heart. We'll discuss more of this later in the book, but recognize that a good financial advisor can help the monetary portion of your retirement plan flow more smoothly and safely. Getting the help of a quality professional can not only provide you with ideas and solutions, but also give you peace of mind. They may also be a good intermediary or mediator during the process of having the talk.

Remember, a critical aspect to ensuring that your parents' best financial interests are covered is that someone other than their financial advisor should know what's going on. You should play an integral part in this partnership. Most quality financial advisors will welcome your involvement in this process.

You should consider the following issues and more when having the talk about financial matters:

1) Do you have a will? If so, when was it last updated?
2) Have you established a trust or another more extensive financial plan?

---

[12] Information on how to choose a financial advisor is available here: http://safe4retirement.com/how-to-pick-a-financial-advisor
[13] US Bank Rate May 2011 study

3) Have you discussed your wishes with the executor of your estate?
4) Do you have a current list of assets, passwords, and important documents and where they are held?
5) Do you have a Durable Power of Attorney designating someone to handle your financial matters if you become incapacitated?
6) Do you have an Advanced Health Care Directive, which allows someone to make your healthcare decisions for you if you become incapacitated? This would include pulling-the-plug decisions, if need be.
7) Do you have a thorough financial plan in place outlining your financial needs, goals, and strategies throughout retirement? And, most importantly, do you review this once a year? This is an area where a quality financial advisor can add enormous value.
8) Do you have long-term care insurance?
9) If you should need to go into an assisted living facility, are you financially capable of doing so?
10) When is the last time you updated the beneficiaries on such things as your retirement accounts, annuities, and life insurance?

Parent/child financial assumptions were part of the 2010 Health Confidence Survey conducted by the Employee Benefits Research Institute. They found that only 42% of adult children knew the approximate amount of their parent's income. On the other hand, 63% of adults *thought* their children knew their income.[14]

If a gap this large exists for just this one subject—income—what other assumption gaps exist for other financial matters? The study also shows that less than half of all children know about their parents' financial status. Having the talk can help to fix this.

---

14 Michele Mintzer, "Assisted Community Living: Having 'The Talk' With Your Parents," Daystar Senior Living Blog, December 6, 2011, http://info.daystarseattle.com/senior-living-blog/bid/73160/Assisted-Community-Living-Having-The-Talk-With-Your-Parents

Physical Health

According to a recent AARP study, only 26% of those between the ages of 65 and 74 years old partake in regular physical activity. It gets worse after the age of 70; only 16% are active regularly. As you'll see in the "Health and Wellness" section later in the book, this is bad news indeed for long-term health.[15]

Common sense tells us that if you don't feel good in retirement, you won't enjoy it as much. Think of how you feel at your current age when you just have a cold or didn't sleep well.

Discussing health with your parents can be a difficult thing. I know it was for me. There are many times I wish I'd discussed with my parents their need to exercise and to involve me in their health decisions. I believe this would have helped them. My hope is that you can learn from my example.

You should understand that the talk includes a myriad of health related issues. They may not be easy to discuss, but there are many ice breakers to help you bring up these topics. Often a health issue for a parent or friend or family member can provide the opportunity. Parents will often look to their educated, and hopefully healthy, child as a resource in discussing the latest in the area of health and eating well.

Because of the many different topic covered in the health section (including healthcare), you'll see many issues overlap between one section and the next. Here's a general sense of what you'll be discussing in this area.

1) Do you have regular physical checkups?
2) Do you participate in aerobic activity at least three times per week, preferably more?
3) Do you have an updated list of all the medications you take?
4) What family member or close friend knows of any existing medical conditions and the treatment for them?

---

15   John Trauth, "Retirement Fitness: How To Shape Up Physically, Psychologically and Financially," Physical Fitness Retirement Golf, http://www.physical-fitness-retirement-golf.com/retirement-fitness.html

5) Have you made absolutely clear to your family members your end-of life wishes? This includes when and if they should terminate life support.
6) As in the financial section, do you have an Advanced Health Care Directive?
7) Are you overweight? If so, do you have a plan for reducing that weight to a healthier level?
8) Do you have stress in your life, and if so, do you have a plan for eliminating as much as possible?
9) How healthy is your diet? (Be honest, now.) Do you eat plenty of fresh fruits and vegetables and stay away from red and processed meats?
10) When your doctor prescribes a treatment in the form of a medication or lifestyle change, do you actually follow his or her instructions?

The body and mind are inextricably intertwined. When you feel good mentally and are happy, you have more energy and want to do more things. When you feel great physically, your mind is clearer and your thoughts more positive.

A happy retirement also means a healthy one. By discussing your plans with your loved ones, they can be part of the process and help out in whatever way possible. This doesn't mean being a burden, it means letting people who care about you know what's going on. This way you also have the opportunity to share all the good things you're discovering in life, too.

Fortunately, you are in control of many aspects of your physical well-being. I'll go into how extensively in the "Health and Wellness" section.

Mental Attitude

As with physical health, it stands to reason that the better your attitude is during retirement and with the overall issue of aging, the more you're going to enjoy yourself. Again, this is an area that needs to be included in the talk.

In their excellent book *Thriving After 55: Your Guide to Fully Living the Rest of Your Life*, authors Henry C. Simmons and E. Craig MacBean discuss many aspects of retirement and aging. One of the most myth-dispelling studies they reference found a positive correlation between aging and happiness.

In their words, "these researchers found that the older the respondents were, the more likely they were to experience positive emotions like cheerfulness, good spirits, and happiness."[16]

I often find that a good way to begin this topic is to ask your parents if they know of anyone whose retirement they would like to emulate. It may be a celebrity, family member, or friend, but this can often lead to a nice discussion about how they would like their retirement to be and how they would like to feel in retirement.

During the talk you should consider the following subjects to include in your discussion about mental attitude.

1) If you're not yet retired, what have you done to prepare yourself for the seismic shift in lifestyle you're about to experience?
2) If you're retired, are you generally happy and looking forward to each day?
3) In general, do you reminisce over positive or negative memories?
4) Do you regularly exercise and eat healthy?
5) Do you give yourself mentally stimulating tasks, like business consulting, crossword puzzles, learning a new language, or taking courses?
6) Do you associate mainly with positive or negative people?
7) Do you find you have a lot of spare time on your hands you don't know what to do with?
8) Are you comfortable with your spirituality?
9) If you're spending the day at home alone, do you shower, shave, and look nice even though no one will see you?

---

[16] Henry C. Simmons and E. Craig MacBean, Thriving After 55: Your Guide to Fully Living the Rest of Your Life, Prime Dynamics LLC, 2000, p. 31

10) If a problem appears on the horizon, do you worry and fret, or do you decide on a solution, act, and then leave it alone?

Being happy with aging is not only possible, but it's also more common than you might think. And there are proactive things you can do to make being happy easy and natural. It's a process that feeds on itself. The better you feel, the more you do and enjoy, and the better you feel.

One thing I've learned in my work with retirement and seeing people live longer and safer in retirement is that attitude is a key driver for success. A positive attitude will often be the difference in living a longer life.

Life should be fun, and there's no reason why their Golden Years should be any different. You can be a major reason for putting fun and joy into your parents' retirement. Your parents want you to be part of their retirement!

Staying Involved

The final key element to the talk is probably the most overlooked. We figure if we have our money in order, we feel good, and haven't yet lost our marbles, then we should be in good shape, right?

Not completely so. More and more research is proving that having rich, positive relationships is a key factor in staying healthy and living longer. We are deeply social creatures, and being consistently alone and uninvolved is contrary to our wiring.

When I wrote my book, *Safe 4 Retirement*, I wanted to understand what causes a surviving spouse to experience broken heart syndrome, which results in their own death soon after that of their spouse. What I learned is that a strong social structure of friends and family is often the best way to survive and become resilient after such a major loss.

This may be an overlooked part of the retirement discussion, but if my experience has taught me anything, it's that this may be the most important part of the discussion. Having your parents thrive in retirement is a joy not only for them but for you as well.

Think about it this way: Your best memories in life probably involve someone other than yourself, too.

The following issues regarding staying involved should be covered in the talk:

1) If you're not yet retired, have you planned on how you'll fill your time when the day comes?
2) Will you stay involved with colleagues from work?
3) What key recreational activities (like golf, croquet, bridge, and opera) do you plan on doing?
4) How involved will you be with your kids and grandkids?
5) What circle of friends do you want to nurture and spend more time with?
6) Will you volunteer in your community or with a national or international organization?
7) What new hobbies will you take up?
8) If you're single, will you look for another life partner?
9) Will you continue to work in your retirement even if you don't need to financially?
10) Will you take classes at a local community center or college?

Retirement and aging should be approached as if this is the reward your parents get for working so hard for all those years. Although much of this in their hands, you can play an important role in making it happen. Help them to expel phrases like "I'm too old for that" and "Not at my age" and "I feel so old." Have your parents replace them with "Shoot, why not!" or "If they can do it, so can I" or "Man, do I feel young for an old fart."

I had a 94-year-old friend who lived on his own, had a feisty 90-year-old girlfriend, and enjoyed what most of us would think of as an active and fruitful life. I heard him complain only once. He'd been diagnosed with a heart ailment and had to go into the hospital for minor surgery. He said mournfully, "If I could just be 80 again, everything would be fine." Now that's a good attitude that you can ask your parents to emulate.

4

How Do I Have the Talk?

Okay, we know why, when, and what to cover during the talk. Now, just how the heck do we go about doing this? Well, the first thing we *don't* want to do is start with something like, "Hey mom, we need to discuss when you'll move into a nursing home, who you're leaving your money and the house to, and what kind of memorial service you want?" Yikes!

Put yourself in your parents' shoes. Most people of their generation were raised never speaking about money or other personal issues except with their spouses. Somewhere along the way it became taboo in our culture, and this only serves to make things more difficult.

Remember, having the talk does not mean controlling anyone's life or giving up control of your own. It also doesn't mean being critical of any situation your parents have found themselves in. If they haven't set themselves up perfectly for retirement and they need some help, don't be judgmental. Just remind yourself of how many times you've turned things on end and hoped no one noticed.

The key word here is *respect*. Congratulate your parents on achieving everything they've done (including creating and raising a brilliant child like yourself). You're here to help in any way you can. In order to help, you first need to understand. This can be a good way to introduce the need for the talk.

Below I've outlined key areas to consider and apply for how to have the talk. Just as going for a swim in a cool ocean, the first plunge is always the hardest. After that, each stroke gets easier, and before you know it, you don't even notice the cold.

Goals

For adult children, before you even begin the talk, make sure your goals are in line with your parents'. It's their money, not yours (even though it may be one day). You're discussing their lives, not yours. This may sound obvious, but it's easy to lose sight of what we're really talking about. A simple reminder of this will help shift the focus directly onto your parents or loved ones, rather than onto yourself.

A good approach is, "I want to make sure I can help you with whatever you need help with."

The end goal is to create a beginning. You're laying the groundwork for further communication, and the information and decisions will happen bit by bit over time. These discussions make it much, much easier.

By having these discussions, you're actually helping to remove a burden from your parents. The reality is that a goal of theirs is to ensure they're able to take care of their family as they get older.

Time the Talk

The talk needs to be timed in two ways. First, as I discussed earlier, adult children should consider what the relative age and well being of their parents is. If they're still working and vital, maybe you can put it off a few years until they're more ready themselves to think of retirement. This is a fine line because you don't want to put it off until a crisis of some sort has already happened.

However, if you're ready to get started, you must also consider the specific timing. The right time is not at Thanksgiving dinner with a table full of people. Nor is it at the county fair barbecue when they're surrounded by friends and acquaintances.

Pick a quiet and comfortable location, and make sure you all have enough time that no one has to jump up and leave. Consider having coffee or lunch together to set the stage.

Address your concerns and tell them you want to help. Clearly explain that no one wants to take control from them. In fact, consider saying, "I need you to stay in charge." It's true. It's their life and their decisions. You're here to help.

You may find that your parents are eager to have this discussion with you and will welcome your initiative to make it happen.

Involve Other Family Members

Do this early and before you have the talk so everyone's concerns can be addressed. It may be effective to designate one person to have the discussions, or you may want to have all siblings there. But remember, you don't want this to feel like an intervention, and you don't want your parents or loved ones to feel like they're being ganged up on.

· Whether you go it alone or with your siblings, your parents will need to be assured that all of their children are aware that this discussion is happening and that everyone is "in sync" with it. The worst thing you can do is to have this discussion without your other family members aware of it. It will cause ill will and put your parents in a bad position. Don't do it alone. The talk is a family matter and must be treated as such.

It's Only a Beginning

Remember, this will be the first of many conversations. You don't have to get everything discussed and agreed upon in one short hour. There's no need to convince anyone of anything. You simply want to get the conversation started so you can revisit it over time.

In fact, the only thing you may accomplish in the first talk is to begin the process. It may require that you leave some information or resources with your parents and ask if you can pick up the discussion at another time after they've had more time to think about what you've said. This is okay!

I've heard from many people that they began the discussion with their parents and after leaving some materials, their parents called them a few weeks later and asked to speak with them further. At that next meeting the parents brought account paperwork, filled out questionnaires, and many wonderful thoughts about how they would like their retirement years to be.

The talk is never a one shot deal. It will take many discussions and should be ongoing. The important part is to take the first step and begin it.

Use an Icebreaker

For some, using an icebreaker is a great way to get the ball rolling. Here are some ideas for segueing into the talk:

- Explain that you and your spouse have just created a will or done some estate planning, and you'd like to tell them about it. Maybe you have questions and need their advice. If you're open about what you're doing, this might make them feel more comfortable about opening up, too.
- If the above doesn't apply, talk about a friend who's in a similar situation. Maybe they're worried about a parent. "My friend Mary's mother isn't recovering well from her surgery and it turns out they haven't done any estate planning at all. Have you and dad talked about this?"
- Discuss something you heard in the news or read in an article or book that raised your concerns.

Be direct. Explain that these have brought up concerns of yours and that you want to talk about them. Again, clarify that you don't want to make any decisions for them, but you do want to understand what they've done about these issues and how you can help. As well, over time you will be able to bring up ideas and issues that they most probably haven't thought of.

Listen

As simple as this sounds, it's often one of our least used communication skills. We live in a get-it-done-fast society, but our parents are entering a stage when their world is slowing down and going inward. Don't pressure your parents to hurry up. Instead, allow for lots of time. And most importantly, listen to what they have to say and want to do.

This will be the time that you'll need the skill of active listening, which basically means that you'll need to be fully engaged in the discussion with your parents. This should include a confirmation of what they've said by recapping it in your own words. This will confirm that you've heard what they're saying and that they've been heard. This is critical to ensure that there have been no misunderstandings or misconceptions.

It's also important that you show "active concern" for both of your parents during the discussion. Don't assume this is something that only your dad has a handle on. You need to ensure that both your dad and mom are actively included in this discussion and that their points of view and opinions have been expressed.

If you don't feel both parents have been effectively heard from, this may require an additional conversation with each parent, and you may find yourself playing an intermediary role. The best approach is to ensure that you hear from each parent when they are together and everyone agrees with what has been said. The skill of active listening will help here.

Be Respectful

Your parents have worked hard to be at the point in their lives where they can successfully consider retiring. This is something to celebrate and be proud of. In the same way that they have been proud of you for your accomplishments throughout your life, you should now be proud of what they have accomplished.

So you need to be respectful of their decisions, opinions, and thoughts throughout this process. Always.

At the end of the day you have no legal right to make any decisions for them. Nor do you have an obligation. What you can do, though, is understand where they are in their financial, health, attitude, and social worlds. If they're not where they want to be or should be, you can help them get there.

Reassure them that you're not going to take away control, but you do have concerns. When talking to your parents, it's good to take note of how David Solie defines control: "A primary human desire at all stages of life that becomes an all consuming driver of behavior in senior adults as they cope with profound losses on a daily basis."[17]

Using this definition, you can see the benefits once again of having the talk at an earlier time in your parents' retirement life. As Solie further points out, the loss of control shows itself as, "the waning of strength, health, peer group members and consultative authority as a person ages, compelling that person to fight to retain whatever does remain under the person's control."[18]

Back Off

The response you get from the first talk will vary. Some parents will resist and feel uncomfortable. "It's all taken care of, don't you worry." Others will share their concerns easily, and the rest will land somewhere in between. Either way, you've opened the door for more conversations.

If they are resistant, back off. Pressuring someone into something is almost never the right move. If you badger them you'll most likely alienate them rather than bring them closer.

Let it rest. See how things go. This will be a process.

You can always revisit the talk again at a later date. This is especially true if a triggering event occurs, like reoccurring missed bills, an accident at home, or the onset of an illness.

Having the talk isn't that difficult, it just seems that way at the beginning. If you keep at the foremost of your mind that you're there to help, not to take anything away from them, this will permeate the conversation.

---

17 David Solie, *How to Say It to Seniors: Closing the Communication Gap with Our Elders*, (Upper Saddle River, NJ: Prentice Hall Press, 2004). Please visit his Web site for more information and valuable resources at http://www.DavidSolie.com.
18 *Ibid.*

We've covered a lot of ground in this first section, and it wouldn't be unusual if you had more questions now then when you started reading. That's just fine. In the next four sections I'll go over the specifics of what should be discussed around each of the Four Keys that will lead to a safe retirement. In each one you'll learn what issues to bring up, and how to address them to find the right end result.

It's my profound belief that both you and your parents will be greatly satisfied with the results of having the talk. These will include a closer relationship between you and your parents, greater certainty that you'll make decisions for your aging parents that are based upon what they truly want, and you'll improve their ability to live a safe retirement.

And a safe retirement means enjoying retirement for as long as possible.[19] If this book can help to accomplish this, it will make both you and your parents happy.

---

19 http://safe4retirement.com/what-is-a-safe-retirement

SECTION TWO

Financial Preparedness and the Talk

5

The Retirement Backdrop

The most natural first step with the talk is discussing whether or not your parents or loved ones have the financial means to retire. Although this is by no means the entire matter signed, sealed, and delivered—a successful retirement entails far more than having enough money—it is certainly a key piece to moving forward.

The problem is that, despite our best intentions and grandest dreams, most pre-retirees in America are woefully underprepared for retirement. Although an estimated 70 million additional baby boomers are expected to retire in the next fifteen years, only 14% of pre-retirees say they are "very confident" they'll have enough money to retire.[20] Not surprisingly, lacking money is a major financial concern for millions of Americans. Many people are navigating the stormy waters of retirement planning and investing their nest egg without proper guidance or planning. This doesn't have to be the case. The talk will smooth out the retirement process and help avoid many pitfalls.

Maybe your retired or pre-retired parents are worried about their retirement plans. Or maybe they're not. If they say they have everything set and there's nothing to worry about, don't just believe them and head out the door. Even if they do have everything set, you and/or another responsible

---

20 Derrick Kinney, ChFC, CASL, CLTC, "Texas Retirement Planning Specialist Derrick Kinney Shows How to Avoid Five Critical Retirement Mistakes," March 16, 2012, press release, http://www.ereleases.com/pr/texas-retirement-planning-specialist-derrick-kinney-shows-avoid-critical-retirement-mistakes-75965

adult needs to know about it. Maybe they've looked into everything and made the right choices, but maybe they haven't. Maybe they received bad advice, overlooked crucial data or potential pitfalls, or simply didn't put the numbers together correctly.

In fact, a recent study has shown that financial literacy begins to drop in the average American when they hit the age of 60. This decline in understanding investments, credit, and other basic money matters continues to erode as people age. However, and here's the clincher, our confidence in our ability to make sound financial decisions *rises* with age.[21] So when we're cruising along in our 60s, 70s, and 80s, thinking we've got this financial bull by the horns, that's when we really should be getting help from a trusted family member and/or a financial professional.

Having the talk with your parents or loved ones helps put this all into perspective. There's no need for them to be concerned, afraid, or uncertain about their financial future in retirement. When handled properly, with a sound and regularly reviewed financial plan, all of you can rest easily. But this is a process you and your parents must be proactive in. Sitting back and hoping for the best is something done when buying lottery tickets, not when planning for your loved ones' Golden Years.

---

21 Michael S. Finke, John S. Howe, and Sandra J. Huston, "Old Age and the Decline in Financial Literacy," Social Science Research Network, August 24, 2011, http://papers.ssrn.com/sol3/papers.cfm?abstract_id=1948627

6

Working with a Professional

In my book *Safe 4 Retirement*, I go into detail about selecting a financial advisor or Certified Financial Planner®.[22] Many of these talented individuals can be a critical source of guidance and objectivity. They are up-to-date on investments and the markets, and they can provide sound retirement planning advice. Well-intentioned golfing buddies or book club members may have adamant opinions about what you should do, but financial advisors are specifically trained to manage money. Don't underestimate their potential value.

One of their biggest advantages is that they become a single point of contact for financial and estate planning. A good financial advisor will act as their financial manager, coordinating portfolios, taxes, estate planning strategies, long-term care, and beneficiaries and decision makers. You and your parents will have the benefit of one key person making sure the puzzle pieces are in place.

Remember, just like in any profession, not all participants are up to speed, and some might not even toe the ethical line. Just like choosing any professional to work with, you must do some due diligence to make sure there's a good fit in talent and personality.

A great place to start is to ask a trusted friend or family member for a referral. Do they have someone they trust and like working with? Have they worked with them comfortably for years? Getting such referrals doesn't al-

---

[22] Go online to www.safe4retirement.com to buy the book and read a selection of related articles.

leviate you from the responsibility or need to interview them, check national databases for their professional records, and compare them with others in their field.

Consider the following for both assessing a new financial advisor and for determining if the one your parents are already working with is the best fit:

- Do they have a good reputation in the local community?
- Are they open about how they're paid? (If not, run.)
- What type of licensing do they have? Can they sell stocks and bonds or are they limited to just mutual funds and insurance products?
- Do they work for a reputable firm, or if they're independent, how long has their platform provider been in operation?
- Do they ask you about your goals and dreams and not just how much money you have?
- Are they trained in creating and maintaining financial plans for retirement?
- How often will they be in contact with you and how often will this be face-to-face?
- Do they conduct annual or biannual reviews?
- Do you "click" with them on a personal or "gut" level?

You want a financial advisor who's willing to put in the time and effort to make sure that your parents have a quality retirement plan. If something doesn't feel right, trust your instincts. Interview several different ones and tell them so. This way they'll know you're serious about the relationship.

Visit the prospective financial advisors with your parents and share your thoughts and gut reactions. A good financial advisor will be open to your involvement as it allows them to create a relationship with you that could extend beyond your parents. They'll understand the value of working with the entire family, and it will facilitate the intergenerational aspect of the talk.

Remember that the best financial advisors are concerned with your entire picture. In a 2012 Merrill Lynch survey, affluent clients were asked,

"What core qualities their financial advisor possesses that keep them loyal to their relationship?" Over half said not only a clear understanding of their financial situation was important, but also that their financial advisor "understood their goals, dreams, and personal values."[23]

The message here is enormous. With a bit of effort, you can find a financial professional who "gets it" and understands that only a holistic view will be the right one for you and your family. Together you and your parents are more than capable of choosing a high quality professional who can keep your loved ones on the right retirement track.

---

23 Merrill Lynch 2012 Affluent Investor Survey

7

Pieces of the Retirement Planning Pie

In the next few chapters I'll be discussing how to evaluate your parent's or loved ones' financial situation. I'll go over assessing where they currently are in regard to money, income, and assets, and specific subjects to consider such as long-term care insurance, moving into senior communities, and the financially eroding effects of healthcare costs.

But before I cover these subjects, it's important to have an understanding of the retirement landscape from a bird's eye view. What's needed financially for retirement? What options do you have to choose from? What specific pitfalls may be lurking that you haven't thought of? Once you understand the pieces involved, you'll be better able to help your parents make the best retirement plan possible.

Keep Your Eye on the Donut

As I will mention again, a successful retirement isn't just a number in a bank account. You can have all the money in the world and still be a miserable grouch. The key is aligning the financial facts with the dreams and goals of your parents. What's on their bucket list? What are their passions and interests? This is the last stage of their lives and should be the best, but the only way to achieve this is to help them live the life that makes them the happiest.

Does that mean cruises to the Caribbean each year? Or a spiffy new mobile home to tour the country at their own pace and schedule? Maybe it just means living comfortably in their own home knowing the bills are paid and the grandkids' birthday presents are well within their budget.

These choices should play a central role in the financial section of the talk. You will bring tremendous value when you align financial capability with dreams and goals. Many times people have a tendency to put their dreams last. They've done it all their lives and by now it's habit. First came work, then came raising a family and work, and now it's retirement. Who has time to take up that painting class or travel to Bhutan or get involved in community theater?

Now, they have all the time in the world and may need to be reminded of it. Ask them what their ideal retirement would look like. What hobbies and activities they would like to pursue? Then build the rest of the financial conversation around including these.

Investment Assets

Typically, when we think of retirement assets, we imagine bank and brokerage accounts brimming with stocks, bonds, and mutual funds. However, in reality these are just one slice of the overall retirement fund pie. Your parents' assets and income will come in a variety of different ways, such as their home, pension plans, social security, insurance products like annuities and life insurance, IRAs and 401(k)s, other real estate, and more.

I'll soon discuss listing your parent's specific assets and sources of income to develop their financial plan. Some they will be able to invest, others they won't. But you'll be listing everything they have of value that could be turned into income.

It's here that a trusted financial advisor can help. The best ones will sit down with you and cover all of these issues, whether the end result makes the financial advisor money or not. They understand that the best way to keep and gain clients is to look after them in the most holistic way possible.

When you discuss investment products with a financial advisor, a good rule of thumb is if you don't understand how it works, don't buy it. This isn't to say you're not bright enough to catch on. On the contrary, the smartest investors (i.e., those that consider risk in relation to reward) shy away from convoluted, complex investments and stick to something else instead—common sense.

Think of it this way. As any chef knows, the best meals in the world come from the freshest, simplest ingredients. The same goes for investments. Quality stocks and bonds in a well-balanced portfolio have historically provided better returns in relation to the risk they give than almost any other investment.

Which brings me to my next subject.

Asset Allocation

As any financial advisor worth his paycheck will tell you, one of the most dangerous portfolios possible is the one with only a few different stocks. In the dot.com boom, I had a client worth well into eight figures, but he absolutely refused to sell any of the company stock that had made him so wealthy. He believed the market pundits who kept raising the target stock price for his company. You can guess the end of this story: He lost nearly everything. If he had diversified his portfolio, he would have kept his wealth and seen it continue to grow.

A well-diversified portfolio is critical to successful investing. When done properly, the portfolio will have a variety of stocks in a diverse array of sectors, mixed with investment grade bonds. These can be in the form of individual securities, mutual funds, or via professional money managers.

The exact ratio of stocks to bonds will vary. A general rule of thumb is to take your age and have that percentage of your portfolio in bonds. Let's say you're 65. Have 65% of your portfolio invested in high-quality bonds. However, given the fact we're living longer and interest rates are so low we'll probably need to get a little more oomph out of our investments. So this ratio errs on the conservative side. But use it as a starting point from which to adjust to your specific situation. Your financial advisor should have suggestions as to optimal ratios.

An important factor in asset allocation is it's a moving target. Not only will the allocation of your investments need to be adjusted as you age, the different sections of your portfolio will need to be rebalanced because they each grow at different rates. This is part of why annual retirement plan reviews are so crucial, and why the talk isn't a one-time occurrence.

How Long Will We Live?

A very important question, indeed. The fact is on average we're living longer and in better health. The past few decades have seen an increased importance on diet and exercise, and a medical community that continues to come up with ways to prevent, treat, and cure diseases.

So how do we allow for this in our retirement planning? Allow for the best; i.e., your parents could live for a very long time. Insurance companies continue to update life expectancy tables. With proper planning, long lifespans can be punched right into the big picture calculation.

Remember that diet and exercise play a huge role in not only the lifespan, but the quality of that life, too. I'll cover this in much more detail in Section Three.

Unexpected Retirement

Unfortunately, this is a more and more common occurrence. With the economic slowdown and continuing layoffs, many people are finding themselves retired whether they want to be or not. The moral of the story is, have the talk with your parents sooner rather than later. Life has a way of "happening," and it's prudent to be prepared.

This doesn't have to mean you and your parents live in a constant state of worry. That's no fun for anyone, and it's bound to be painful. It means have the talk, get things in order, and then forget about it. Sit down together once a year for an annual review, and then forget about it again. This is the key to prudence in league with happiness.

Women and the Financial Talk

Women have certain issues that need to be addressed during the talk. First of all, in a typical household, the job of handling the money and bills tends to fall to one spouse or the other. Interestingly, it's 50-50 as to whether it will be the husband or wife. What this means, though, is that if your father was the one who paid the bills, your mother might not have a clue about the family finances.

The problem is women tend to live longer and are more likely to be the one widowed. It's crucial you get her involved in the talk, even if you have to coax her into it. She may have no interest, so it's your job to explain why it's so important. Or, she may be very interested but has no background in finances or investing if she wasn't the one handling the bills.

On top of this, it's not uncommon for the wife to have been the one to raise the children. If this was the case, she would have had less time to build up a career and, therefore, have lower social security benefits coming in. All these are issues you need to consider in the talk.

A survey conducted by Merrill Lynch found that, in general, women "tell us they do not feel well served by the wealth-management industry, and that the relationship with the advisor is typically with the husband, which is why, when the husband dies, and the assets go to the wife, the typical advisor keeps those assets only 46 percent of the time."[24]

From this point on, make sure both spouses are equally involved in all aspects of the talk. It's only fair and will keep the retirement planning you do on a steady track no matter which spouse passes away first.

Blended Families

With divorce a common occurrence, it's no wonder more and more families are made up of second or third marriages, and often include children from different spouses. In the context of financial planning and the talk,

---

24 http://newsroom.bankofamerica.com/speeches/wealth-investment-management/remarks-investment-company-institutes-annual-meeting-krawcheck

this is an area with enormous potential for misunderstandings and false expectations.

What's the best preventative medicine? Get it out in the open during the talk. If you're the lead person helping your parents or loved ones, then you need to gently broach the subject of how they want to handle this diverse array of people. They may have thought it out, but then they might not have. You're there to help and provide guidance if necessary.

While you may be the person bringing up the subjects and heading the talk, it's important to involve everyone at some point along the way. This will avoid any potential misunderstandings down the road.

When One Spouse Dies

Whether or not you've had the talk at this point, when one spouse dies the survivor will be in a world of hurt and confusion. The loss of one's spouse is one of life's most devastating events. Even if they had everything organized financially and a plan in place, the surviving spouse won't be thinking clearly. Or, the worst-case scenario, maybe you haven't yet had the talk and their financial world is a complete mystery to both the surviving spouse and you.

While certainly not comprehensive, the following is a list of actions you can gradually take to help ease the burden of this emotional time. Your presence and guidance will most probably bring enormous relief to the survivor during this traumatic time.

- Advise the surviving spouse to not make any major financial decisions, like selling the primary home, for a full year. Mourning is an emotionally taxing process. Let them take time to gradually come out of the fog.
- Notify their financial advisor, lawyer, CPA, and any other professional they're working with. Meet with each to revise estate, financial, and tax planning.
- Check that the monthly bills are being paid. The surviving spouse may not have been in charge of this.

- Make sure to cancel any premiums on life or health insurance in the name of the deceased. I've seen far too many cases where the insurance companies kept receiving automatic payments for months afterwards.
- Order at least ten death certificates, and possibly more. For some bizarre reason, they're much more difficult to get the longer you wait. You'll need them for a variety of reasons.
- Collect life insurance benefits.
- Collect any social security benefits the survivor is eligible for.
- If the spouse was employed, contact the employer for any retirement funds to roll over. These may be in the form of a pension plan, 401(k), stock options, deferred compensation, etc.
- Change the name to the survivor on any beneficiary accounts, such as IRAs.
- Make sure the survivor tells you of any investments he or she is considering becoming involved in. Unscrupulous sales people prey on the recently widowed as easy targets for a quick sale.

Identity Theft

As if all of that isn't enough, now we get to worry about someone "borrowing" our social security numbers or credit card information to make their own purchases with our money. Although identity theft is common enough to take precautions against, your parents or loved ones might not be taking all the necessary steps to protect their identity and assets against cyber-thieves.

The following steps can help make sure identity theft is scratched from the list of potential problems:

- Buy a shredder and get your parents to use it for anything that has personal data on it.
- Check that neither of your parents have their social security card, pin numbers, or passwords in their wallet or billfold.

- If they're doing online banking, make sure they only use reputable sites. Two clues are an "s" after the "http" in the Web site address, and the little yellow lock that appears in the lower tool bar.

- Warn them about "phishing" e-mails that appear to come from the bank or financial institution but are just devious ways to get them to give out their personal information.

- Have them mail any letters with personal details, such as their social security number or account details, from a post office collection box rather than from an unguarded personal mailbox, which is a convenient way for the bad guys to steal your information.

- Keep copies of their credit cards, social security cards, and other important documents. If a credit card is stolen, they'll have the correct phone numbers at hand to cancel the cards.

- Encourage them to monitor their bank statements regularly. This way if any suspicious charges come up, they can act immediately.

- Remind them that cell phones, iPads, and other cool technology are also great targets for thieves. We live in a world now where someone can walk by your outdoor Starbucks table and swipe your cell phone without you even noticing.

8

The Financial Plan

While working together with a financial professional is usually the best option for creating a financial plan, much of the groundwork can and should be done beforehand. Whether or not you seek professional advice, you will need the following information.

The basic premise of a financial plan isn't that wild a concept. At its most fundamental, it's all about comparing the inflow and outflow of money over a long period of time. I'll be asking you to organize what assets your parents have that can be used toward retirement (not all assets can). Next we list all debt. To this side of the balance sheet we also list the expenses. Finally, we add a touch of inflation and see what the numbers turn out to be.

The result is a view of the overall financial landscape. What's left over after allowing for anticipated expenses and an emergency savings fund we allocate to dreams and goals and, sometimes, to inheritances. However, inheritances are diminishing in size and frequency. According to a Merrill Lynch survey in 2011, of those investors with over $250,000 in investable assets, only 41% said leaving an inheritance was a top concern for them.[25]

The reasons for this are twofold. First, the economic slowdown has left a dent in many retirees' portfolios. Parents are simply no longer *able* to give as much away. Second, and perhaps the more powerful reason, is what I had mentioned above in describing generational differences. For baby boomers

---

25 The Wall Street Journal, *Counting on an Inheritance? Count Again*, by Anne Tergesen, June 11, 2012.

it's become more important to them to leave behind a legacy rather than money. It's a matter of different values coming into play.

We all want to know we're more important than a dollar sign or random number. We want to believe that our impact on this world was most powerful on the people we met and whose lives we changed for the better. This is the power of a legacy, and its importance is amplified as we age.

Keep this in mind when you have the talk about retirement planning. The most important issue may not be the numbers at the bottom of the balance sheet for them. Of course, they need to be able to afford to retire and live comfortably, but once that's covered, it's the impact they had on the world and what their lives meant that may be most important.

All these needs can be uncovered and dealt with as a result of the talk. You can use existing worksheets or you can simply take a pencil and paper and go through the next section with your parents (or have them do it on their own and then share it with you later).

Setting the Stage

By this stage of the talk, you should have reached an agreement with your parents that you're going to sit down together and go through the nitty-gritty of their financial world. If you followed the advice I outlined in Section One, they will understand that you're here not to take control, but to make sure that *they* have control over their financial future.

Knowledge is power, and the more knowledge they have over their finances and choices, the more powerful they become. You're the facilitator. You're their advocate down the twisted alleyways of money and markets. If that makes you shiver in your boots, don't worry. I'll walk you through what comes next.

In preparation for forming a financial plan, or preparing the data for a professional to do so, make sure your parents understand the degree of detail you'll be going into. You'll need to know everything about their assets, liability, income, and expenses. I used to do this for a living and although it sounds like a lot, it goes smoothly once you get your teeth into it. But my point is, make sure your parents are ready for digging deep. We're not removing a wart; we're going in for open-heart surgery!

Remember, all of this can be made easier with the help of a good financial advisor. You'll still need to provide the numbers, but they're trained to crunch them.

Let's begin!

Assets and Income

First, we'll start with the fun stuff—what your parents have that can be used toward retirement. Organize the data on paper or on a computer, whichever your parents will find easiest to work with. Many financial planning software programs exist where you simply plug in the answers to questions asked—much like TurboTax.

We'll want to separate these assets into two categories: those that can be used toward retirement more or less immediately, and those that would need to be sold first, like the family home. We certainly don't want to make a financial plan based on the idea that your parents have to be uprooted from where they live. That's a last resort option or something to be considered as they find maintaining a home more and more difficult. I cover this in more detail below.

So begin by listing all assets that can be turned into some form of income, such as

- retirement accounts, like IRAs, 401(k)s, and other defined contribution plans
- investment accounts (these will differ from the above in that the proceeds are taxable, as opposed to tax deferred)
- savings and checking accounts
- pension plan income
- Social Security income
- real estate income, such as rentals

- employment income, in the case that one or the both of them plan on working at least part-time during retirement
- income from dividends, oil leases, or other investments
- anything else you and they can think of

Next, make a list of all the other assets they have and their values, such as:

- the family home
- a second home or other family property
- jewelry, paintings, and/or antiques
- any other illiquid assets

The issue is the first list will be what they actually use to retire with. The second list will be of items of value, but those that most likely will be passed on in an inheritance and sold only if necessary.

Liabilities and Expenses

Not as much fun but equally important is the discussion about debt and expenses. These expenses should be those that are fixed or generally anticipated. Funds for dreams and goals come in the next section. I'll also discuss long-term care and medical expenses in more detail below.

Many people pay off their mortgage when they retire. The logic here is to keep monthly expenses to a minimum; also, the tax deductions aren't as helpful when you're making far less of an annual income. This is definitely an option you should consider and an area where a good financial advisor can help. He or she will be able to plug in the numbers either way and directly compare the two financial outcomes.

Other than the mortgage payment, the rule of thumb is that living expenses in retirement will be 80% of those during working years. The logic here is that less money is spent on such things as gas, cars, commuting, business clothes, and lunches out. Life is cheaper when you settle into your retirement routine at home. Now, as for those of you who plan on three cruises a year, memberships at new golf courses, and weekly gourmet dinner parties, well … maybe 80% isn't your number. Consider it a guideline within which to work.

For general expenses consider the following:

- regular monthly expenses such as utility bills, food, clothes, and dues (use the 80% figure if that helps)
- mortgage payments (include those for a second home if relevant)
- home equity line of credit
- credit card payments or any other loan payments (including student loans)
- car payments including leases
- property taxes and any other taxes owed
- a family member needing help
- regular charity contributions
- any other debt or expenses

Also make note of the interest rate they're paying on any debt. This is a good time to consider refinancing or otherwise lowering those rates if the debt is going to be held.

The Path Ahead

At this point you have a clear idea of what assets and liabilities exist in your family's financial world. You know what type of income they're receiving and what debt payments they have.

Now comes the number crunching, and you can do this yourself or hire a professional. Computer software makes this a breeze. The key is to accurately record the inflow and outflow, where each is coming from, and what, if any, adjustments need to be made to give your parents the maximum income they can realize with the most minimal impact on their savings. Be sure to add at least a 3% inflation rate for expenses.

From this you will understand how much they have left over for dreams and goals. Once the basics have been taken care of, the rest is for making the Golden Years shine.

Be very careful about tapping into actual retirement fund principal. This is the goose that lays the golden income egg. When you chip away at that, you chip away at their income power, something to be done reluctantly and only with the understanding of how that may impact future income.

And always—always!—allow for potholes in the road of life. An emergency fund is critical to a safe retirement. What happens if unexpected medical expenses arise for one of your parents or another family member? Or a house or car bill occurs that isn't covered by insurance? Life has a way of happening. It's best to allow for the worst to happen, but hope it never does.

Going Back to Work

One option for increasing income during retirement is to do the opposite—go back to work! Okay, settle down. It doesn't have to be that bad.

The reasons for working during retirement are twofold. First, some people like to stay intellectually stimulated and active through working part-time or consulting. This is their primary motivation.

Second, some people need the extra income for living expenses or just until they become eligible for Medicare. The work can be part-time. It can also be in a new field that might provide more opportunity for growth or interests. Maybe you love golf, so take up a part-time job in the pro shop at the local public course. Maybe you've been managing a household all your life and are happy to take over the books for a young couple's new business. Think of it as an opportunity to experience new things while bringing in extra funds.

For more information on finding jobs and working as a senior, see Section Five, "Staying Involved."

When to Claim Social Security

Your parents have a choice as to when they claim Social Security. If the income side of the balance sheet is a little short, they can choose to begin their Social Security payments at the age of 62. If both spouses are living, one can claim his or hers earlier, and the other can begin later. It's important to understand the different alternatives.

If they claim benefits at age 62, the amount they receive will be approximately 20% less than it would be normally at full retirement. Conversely, if they wait until they're 70, they'll receive much more than they would if they claimed their benefits at their normal retirement age (currently 65). This math is all based on the Social Security Administration's life expectancy tables and is meant to average out to equal total amounts.

Other forms of benefits are available through Social Security, such as survivor's benefits for the surviving spouse. The key is to take these alternatives into consideration during the talk. If your parents need a bit more money when they're younger, they can claim earlier. If they don't, then why not wait until they get the maximum benefit at 70?

Estate Planning

The final step in a sound financial plan is estate planning. You'd be amazed at how many well-off couples and individuals I've worked with who didn't even have a will. These are folks worth millions who through the profound effects of inertia would have left the fate of their life savings up to the state. Not a pretty thought.

Everyone needs a will; many others may need more extensive estate planning. Even if you have a modest amount of assets and few survivors, if any, do you want the state to decide what happens when you die? Most of us would rather make those decisions ourselves.

The opportunities are enormous. Maybe your parents would like to help out their children financially while they're building their careers, and then give the rest of their assets to charity when they die. Maybe they'd like to start a foundation and don't have a clue where to begin. Or maybe they don't want you to know how they're going to divvy up their world when they pass. The issue is to get them in front of a good estate attorney so they can turn those wishes into realities.

The talk will create the scene for this to happen. It can be awkward to discuss inheritances when your parents are still alive and thriving. It can seem like you want something from them when that's the last thing in your mind. But it's by having a talk that you can clarify all of these matters.

Begin by asking them what they have in place already; i.e., do they have a will? If so, when was it last updated? In many states, such as California, a Revocable Living Trust is essential for most estates over $100,000, including the primary residence. If you know anything about real estate values in California, then you understand this means nearly everyone needs more than a will.

The best solution is to find out what your parents have already done, and then encourage them to visit with an estate attorney, with or without you.

Annual Review

It's difficult to overstate the value of this one step. Financial plans, like investment portfolios, are moving targets. The only thing certain in life is that things will *not* stay the same. Change is inevitable and, therefore, financial plans need to be monitored and updated. Fortunately, the process is easy.

If you're working with a good financial advisor, he'll be one step ahead of you and is already planning annual reviews. However, if you're doing the planning on your own, then you'll need to mark it on your calendar. Any date will do. If you mark it for every March 1, than reviewing the previous year's financial plan could be part of your annual spring cleaning.

Begin by asking if anything has changed in their lives that has or will have a financial impact. Make sure the expenses never exceed the revenue, and that all debt is being paid off, refinanced, or both. In a nutshell, is the plan working? If not, what changes do you all need to make so that it does work?

A Safe Retirement annual review will also include making sure your parents are staying healthy through their diet and exercise, that their mental attitude is sharp and positive, and that they're involved with people they care about. I'll get into each of these in more detail in the upcoming sections.

9

Long Term Care

Rosalyn Carter wasn't joking when she said, "There are only four kinds of people in the world: those who have been caregivers, those who are currently caregivers, those who will be caregivers and those who will need caregivers."[26]

On any given day, over 65 million people in America spend at least part of their day in the role of caregiver for someone ill or disabled. We all age, and the vast majority of us will one day need a caregiver. The question is, who will do it and how will we pay for it?

The National Family Caregivers Association estimates that over $306 billion in unpaid caregiving occurs every year. Not surprising given the majority of caregiving is done by family members (folks like you and me). Some estimates state that the average working caregiver loses $600,000 in income over his or her lifetime due to the loss of income, promotion opportunities, and other employment benefits.[27]

This is no small potatoes. On the other hand, as a caregiver, you're able to be there for those you love in their time of need. The value of this is immeasurable and varies for each one of us.

Most of us, however, don't want to think of ourselves as burdens to those we love. The thought of my children having to wipe the drool from my lips

---

26 National Family Caregivers Association, www.nfcacares.org.
27 Steve Weisman, *Boomer or Bust: Your Financial Guide to Retirement, Health Care, Medicare, and Long-term Care*, Pearson, Prentice Hall, 2007, p. 100.

and change my diapers makes me cringe. It inspires me to think of other alternatives, as I've been coaching my clients for years.

So given that your parents will probably need caregiving at some stage in their lives, what are the choices you can bring up during the talk?

- offer to roll up your sleeves when the time comes and do the job yourself
- pay for homecare and eventually a nursing home out-of-pocket
- revert to Medicaid.
- use the value of their primary residence to pay for professional caregiving at home or in a facility.
- long-term care insurance to pay for professional caregving

Let's look at these individually.

Becoming the Caregiver Yourself

Whether based on money or a sense of duty or both, being the primary caregiver is a deeply personal decision. You will be doing a great service at no small cost to yourself. However, many families will have it no other way. So during the talk, make sure your parents understand what hard work caregiving is. This doesn't turn you into a whiner; it means the reality is out in the open. It's hard work!

From a financial perspective several options exist. If your parents are low-income, you may have to shoulder the financial burden yourself. Otherwise, consider asking them to pay you for your caregiving to offset the loss of employment income. You can also hire professional caregivers to give you time to go to work and time to have a normal life.

In the beginning this may all seem easy. But remember, your parents will only need more caregiving in the future, not less. For support, ideas, and caregiver communities, reach out to national caregiving groups, such as

- National Family Caregivers Association, www.nfcacares.org
- National Alliance for Caregiving, www.caregiving.org

- National Association for Home Care, www.nahc.org
- Family Caregiver Alliance, www.caregiver.org

Paying Out-of-Pocket

First, let's look at estimates of current costs. According to Anna Rappaport Consulting, these are the 2010 averages:[28]

- $205/day is the national average daily rate for a semi-private room in a nursing home
- $21/hour is the average for a home health aide
- $67/day is the average for day care in an adult health center
- $3,293/month is the average to live in an assisted living facility

Do the math. It's not cheap. But if your parents can afford these types of bills for possibly many years to come, then this is a viable alternative. Remember to factor in inflation.

Medicaid

This is sometimes what happens after the funds run out from the strategy above. Medicaid is the government health insurance program for qualifying low-income individuals and families. Nursing home care is included.

Medicaid is funded at both the state and federal level, but the qualifying criteria varies from state to state. Generally, to qualify for Medicaid's aged health care services, you must be 65 or older, have no assets, and have limited extended family support. So if you are able to pay for your parents' caregiving, they will probably not be eligible for Medicaid.

In a nutshell, check out your state's rules, but generally this is a last resort option.

Using the Primary Home as Funding

Depending on the value of the home, this can be a viable, option, though not always an attractive one. Your parents can sell their home and use the proceeds to fund home health care, assisted living, and/or nursing home care.

---

28 Anna Rappaport Consulting, "Helping People Make Better Retirement Decisions: Resources From the Society of Actuaries," Webcast for RIIA, January 2012. Available online at http://www.soa.org/files/research/.../research-helping-people-webcast.pdf.

Obviously, they need to make sure the home is worth enough to cover all these costs, as it's impossible to predict exactly how long one will live. So while feasible, this plan has definite limitations.

Long-Term Care Insurance

This is the most attractive option, in my opinion. The earlier your parents apply for long-term care, the lower the premiums and the more quickly this safety umbrella springs into place. So, the sooner your parents investigate this option, the better. This is the ideal solution for those who don't have enough money to self-insure (i.e., pay for the expenses out-of-pocket), but do have more than would ever qualify them for Medicaid. Another reason to have the talk early!

This option is also ideal for those who want to leave a financial inheritance behind. The idea of spending all their hard-earning money on healthcare just doesn't make that much sense to many people. They'd rather let their children and grandchildren, or a favorite charity or foundation, reap the benefits of their hard work. Long-term care insurance provides peace of mind that they can finish out their days in comfort while also leaving behind a financial legacy.

As with so many aspects of financial planning, finding a quality long-term care provider is a job your financial advisor should be able to easily do. Various clauses, benefits, waiting periods, and premiums will apply, and your financial advisor can help walk you through them. In a nutshell, this insurance will pay for a variety of homecare and nursing home options depending on the type you buy. The earlier your parents buy it, the better (the premiums will be lower), and you can very wisely include an inflation rider so the amount of daily coverage you're eligible for will increase over the years.

I have seen friends and family members who developed health problems and didn't have either long-term care insurance or the financial means to pay for their healthcare bills. It is simply an ugly but very real aspect of our society that if you don't plan for significantly higher healthcare costs as you age, you can be financially cleaned out and left in a state-run home. I have yet to meet a person who's found that option attractive.

Another facet to the problem is it can drain the financial resources of younger generations, too. I know a middle-aged couple whom I'll call John and Nancy. John's parents hadn't saved much money but were doing fine on Social Security and a small pension. They had a small apartment in Florida where they were happy.

However, that was until John's mother needed an extended hospital stay, and his parents realized they had both became too old and frail to live on their own. John and Nancy worked full-time and lived on the opposite side of the country. But they both loved John's parents and couldn't bear to see them living on their own when they needed extra help. Although it wasn't realistic for his parents to live with them, John helped pay for his parents to live in an assisted living facility. The problem was, as his parents' aged, the amount of care they needed increased. And so did John's bills. Before long he was spending thousands of dollars a month on his parents' care and tapping into the savings he and Nancy had built for their own retirement. John and Nancy found themselves in the uncomfortable "sandwich" of trying to save for their own retirement while paying for the care of his parents.

If John's parents had bought long-term care insurance this debacle never would have happened. (I met John when his parents were too old to be eligible for long-term care insurance.) What we can take from this unfortunate story is the knowledge that long-term care insurance doesn't just help your parents, it helps you, too.

Consider purchasing a Survivorship Rider with the long-term care policy. Although, this will cost your parents more in monthly premiums, the benefit is that if one of them dies, the long-term care insurance premiums for the other are paid up in full. This is an awesome option, but be sure to do the math and make sure that the insurance premium with the rider (which will cost extra) is worth the value of the surviving spouse having no premium at all.

Purchasing an Inflation Rider should almost be considered mandatory. As healthcare costs continue to rise, your parents will need to rest assured that the benefits of their long-term care insurance will continue to cover the increased costs.

Another factor to consider is if both parents are living, it will be cheaper to buy a policy together. Usually, one spouse cares for the other for a certain period of time. This saves the insurance company money and they know it.

You may have read about how forming an irrevocable trust can protect assets from being required to be used for healthcare costs. This can be a viable alternative, but remember there's now a five-year look back provision. Any assets you include in the trust can be required to be used for Medicaid expenses up until they've been in the trust for five years. (That number keeps changing, so be sure and check for the latest figure.)

10

Moving From the Family Home

Studies and common sense alike have shown that selling the family home and moving into a senior living facility can be one of the most traumatic experiences in life. Years of family, children, scraped knees, pets, laughter, tears, and everything in between get all knotted up in this one place. For your parents, selling their home can be like selling their lives away.

I had a family member who lived to the age of 103, all the while living in her own home. However, this is the exception to the rule. Most of us will at some point either move in with our children, or retire to a senior living facility of some type.

Eventually, you will need to broach this subject with your parents. Take into consideration this powerful emotional connection when you have the talk.

It's not even just a matter of leaving behind memories (which they won't, they'll take them right along with them in their minds), it's also an admission of losing power. If you remember from Section One, the loss of power is one of the most uncomfortable facets of aging. Nobody likes it, and that power doesn't come back.

However, this entire subject can be flipped on its head and seen as the positive event it is. Caring for a home is a lot of hard work; in fact, it can be a pain in the butt. We all know that. It's getting our minds around the alternative that's the issue.

Senior living facilities come in a variety of forms and degrees of "assistance." Let's look at several types.

Senior Living Communities

These communities of individual homes and/or apartments all have one thing in common: they restrict the age of members and, therefore, those who can live within the community, usually starting somewhere between 55 and 65. Some even have restrictions as to how long children can visit (for example, one week at a time and no more).

The advantages are that residents live among people of their own age who are all near or in retirement. Often there's an active social scene with dozens of clubs, workshops, committees, and sports for members. From golf to scrapbooking to poker to mah jong, chances are there will be an active group. This can be a great way to keep busy and socially active during retirement. You'll read in Section Five how important staying involved is for your parents as they age.

The disadvantages are when it comes time for your parents to receive more daily assistance (meals cooked, medicines accounted for, etc.), they will need to move again. However, senior communities can be a great bridge between selling the family home and moving into a more comprehensive living facility.

Assisted Living Centers

The types of assisted living facilities available can seem infinite, and they darn near are. Various levels of assistance are provided, as are extra activities and on-site medical care. At first glance, choosing one can seem like quite the daunting task. Fortunately, the government has an excellent Web site that can help you sift through the alternatives, www.eldercare.gov. Another source of help is www.AssistedLivingFacilities.org.

Generally, residents live in apartments with kitchens, and have the option of two or three cooked meals in a communal cafeteria. Social activities are coordinated, as are buses to and from banks, shops, doctors' offices, movie theaters, hairdressers, and generally wherever residents want to go within reason.

One key difference lies in the amount of medical attention provided and allowed for. Laws come into play here. A lower-level facility will not have registered nurses or physicians on-site, but will have aides who can help dispense medicine and assist with some daily living activities.

Facilities with higher levels of care provide increased medical capabilities, but at a higher cost. Costs themselves will vary by state, quality, and level of assistance. The national average in 2012 was $3,300 per month.[29]

When having the talk about assisted living with your parents, make sure they understand the upside. They'll be living with other retired people with boatloads of life experiences and history. All those home chores like gardening, fixing the roof, chasing off raccoons, whatever, will be taken care of for them. Instead, they can spend time doing what they love while living in a comfortable and secure environment. They're no longer "living alone."

Have them be active participants in choosing the right assisted living facility. The style and feel vary considerably and many are pretty attractive places. Interview staff, talk to residents, wander the halls, and take in the feel. How clean is it? What does it smell like? Even eat a meal in the cafeteria to check out the cooking. All these factors add up to helping you and your parents make the best choice.

Nursing Homes

The next highest level of care is a nursing home. Far more medical attention is usually available. At this point your loved one needs a much greater amount of care than either yourself or an assisted living facility can provide. Sometimes assisted living facilities and nursing homes will be part of the same company and property. When a resident reaches a point where he or she needs nursing home care, it's right there.

Nursing homes can be accredited by either Medicare and/or Medicaid, which means they've passed a state assessment. Also check if it's accredited by the Joint Commission on the Accreditation of Healthcare Organizations (JCAHO)[30] This nonprofit organization helps assess and evaluate nursing homes and is a great source of information.

---

29 http://www.AssistedLivingFacilities.org
30 http://www.jcaho.org

When having the talk, mention the possibility of your parents ever needing a nursing home and if they have any wishes regarding this. The thought can be scary, so tread carefully. Often the location of the home is important so family members and friends can easily visit. Also, is it close to their primary physician? What services and activities are provided and what's the general feel of the place? Take the time to carefully consider the options.

Life Changes

The one constant in life is change. During the talk about relocating from the family home, make sure you accentuate the positive. Be sensitive to the wealth of emotions tied to the event, but also talk about being realistic. At a certain point in life it doesn't make sense to have the burden of looking after your own home.

The downside of losing this type of control can be offset by the increased access to interesting people, activities, medical help, and the freedom from all that work of looking after your home.

11

Government Help

No matter what your opinions are about the size and reach of government programs, there are some government services that do exist to help you and your loved ones in their senior years.

Social Security is one such service that I've already discussed, and it can be a significant form of income for many in their retirement years. For our purposes here, Social Security is easy to deal with because it's on the income side of the balance sheet. Your parents have paid into it all their lives, and now in retirement they receive a steady income back. Other government services aren't so simple.

Medicare and Medicaid are also government-funded systems our tax dollars have been financing. After the age of 65 (and earlier for Medicaid in some cases), many of our medical expenses are taken care of through one of these two services—but not all of them. The cost of healthcare is rising in America for everyone. During the financial planning segment of the talk, you will need to allow for these costs and how they will impact your loved ones.

The problem is that no one knows what the future will hold. President Barack Obama's healthcare plan passed through Congress, but healthcare can change over time depending on elections and the day-to-day dynamics of the legislative process. We simply don't know how healthcare costs will evolve over the next few years, much less the next few decades.

What we can do is move forward with the situation as it stands, knowing government systems change regularly, but slowly. This will be a good starting place to base future plans on.

I'd like to go more thoroughly into Medicare and what costs may be associated with these healthcare services.

An important point to make is an obvious one. The healthier we are, the lower our healthcare costs because we simply don't have that many issues that need to be addressed. In the next section I extensively cover having a healthy retirement and how you can facilitate this in the talk. You'll also learn how you can be healthier yourself, as you'll eventually be taking this retirement road, too.

Medicare

Medicare is our existing national health care system. To qualify you must be eligible for Social Security and at least 65 years old or disabled. It comes in four parts, cleverly named A, B, C, and D. Let's look briefly at each one.

Part A is hospital insurance and you are automatically enrolled in this service when you join Medicare. It covers hospital stays, some home healthcare, and hospice care. If you are eligible for full Social Security benefits (that is, you have forty quarters or more of employment where you paid Social Security), then Part A is free. If you have less than forty quarters then you could pay up to $451 a month.[31]

You are also required to pay a deductible for hospital stay costs and certain co-pays apply. So, it's not quite free. Check out the government's Medicare Web site for the latest on costs.[32]

Part B is voluntary and covers medical insurance. Doctor's fees, outpatient care, ambulance services, mental health services are a few of the benefits. You pay a monthly premium depending on your income. In 2012 this premium ranged from $99.90 to $319.70, the lower fee being charged to the lower income folks.[33]

---

31 http://www.medicare.gov/cost/.
32 Ibid.
33 Ibid.

Part C is also called Medicare Advantage and is offered by private companies approved by Medicare. HMOs (Health Maintenance Organizations) and PPOs (Preferred Provider Organizations) contract with Medicare to provide all of your Part A and B services. They may also offer vision, hearing, and dental programs, and most will also include prescription drug plans (Part D).

The costs associated with Part C plans include your normal Part B premium, plus an additional premium depending on the Medicare Advantage plan you choose. You may also be responsible for deductibles and co-pays as you would with Parts A and B.

Part D is the prescription drug plan, and here, too, private companies work with Medicare to provide different prescription drug plans. Each will have a different set of benefits and restrictions.

What we've learned is Medicare isn't completely free. Although extensive healthcare services are offered, additional services, such as Part C (Medicare Advantage) and Part D (prescription drug coverage), can also be purchased.

Whew! I didn't say it was going to be straightforward!

Now let's look more closely at some additional costs.

Gaps exist in the coverage provided by Medicare Parts A and B. Also, the deductibles and co-pays can add up and, before long, this national healthcare service is costing a pretty penny.

To solve these gaps in coverage and expenses not paid, insurance called Medigap came into play. Again, these are private insurance companies, approved by Medicare, whose coverage fills the "gaps." Currently, 12 such policies have been approved and are also cleverly named alphabetically, A through L.

Choosing which Medigap plan is right for your parents is quite a process. However, certain considerations will help narrow down your choices. First, if you elect to go with a Medicare C plan (Medicare Advantage), then some of the gaps in coverage and expensive co-pays might be taken care of—depending on the plan, of course. But look into this, as you don't want to be paying for double coverage.

Next, several Medigap plans offer prescription drug coverage to cover another gap in the Medicare system—this one's called the "donut hole." But if your Medicare Part C covers the donut hole, then you won't need any Medigap plan that does the same thing.

The infamous donut hole gap occurs with Part D, Medicare's prescription drug plan. Although prescription drugs are covered, participants are responsible for specific out-of-pocket expenses that increase each year.

First, the participant is responsible for paying a deductible, which in 2012 is $320. Coverage is then extended until a certain threshold is reached; in 2012 this is $2,930. The participant pays 25% of this amount. After this amount is reached in total costs, the participant is then responsible for *all* prescription drug costs until the catastrophic portion of the benefit kicks in and begins again covering costs. This total gap, or donut hole, is $4,700 in 2012.

This is what it looks like:

$320.00	=	deductible; plus
$652.50	=	25% of $2,930; plus
$3,737.50	=	coverage gap (the donut hole).
$4,700.00	=	the maximum out-of-pocket cost prior to catastrophic coverage kicking in[34]

Ugly, isn't it?

However, this coverage gap and expense can be covered in Part C, Medicare Advantage programs, and with Medigap insurance policies.

Other gaps in coverage exist along with more out-of-pocket expenses. Each year these amounts increase. While we don't know fully how "Obamacare" will affect this issue yet, it's wise to allow for these expenses and carefully consider which policies to buy to avoid spending excess money on healthcare. Add any new insurance premiums to your financial plan.

---

[34] http://www.q1medicare.com/PartD-The-2012-Medicare-Part-D-Outlook.php

In Summary

As I mentioned above, a great way to reduce healthcare costs is for your parents to stay as healthy as possible. Not only is this financially sound, but it's a lot more fun, too. No one wants to go through life feeling poorly.

In the next section, I cover what actions you and your parents can take to have a healthy and safe retirement. Although it is not as obvious, this part of the talk is equally important as the financial aspect, or any other. Most importantly, it is possible to take control of your health and wellness and be an active participant in how you feel physically. It's not all "in the genes." Through the right diet and proper exercise, health can improve, disease could be avoided, and a general feeling of well-being created and maintained.

Section Three

Physical Health and the Talk

12

The Incredible Cost-Saving Benefits of a Walk in the Park

A recent Fidelity Investments report stated that "a 65-year-old couple retiring this year without any employer-based health coverage would need an estimated $240,000 to cover medical costs through retirement."[35]

This shocking statistic flies in the face of the standard misconception that once we "go on Medicare" our medical expenses will be taken care of. The Fidelity report is based on a 65-year-old couple who is already covered by Medicare, and takes into account the premiums, deductibles, co-insurance, and prescription drug costs involved. It also includes vision and hearing expenses.

What the cost estimate doesn't cover—in other words, those bills that would be on top of the $240,000—are dental services, over-the-counter drugs (such as aspirin), and long-term care. In short, the cost of healthcare is a continuing financial concern that is best planned for as early as possible.

The good news is that with a bit of proactive thought and action, we can become healthier individuals and, therefore, lower and/or delay these costs.

According to David Solie, there's a huge difference between what *makes* us healthy, and what we *spend* on being healthy.

---

35 Ann Carrns, "New Estimate Sees Rise in Medical Costs in Retirement," *The New York Times*, May 9, 2012.

What Makes Us Healthy?

50% = Healthful Behaviors

20% = Our Environment

20% = Our Genes

10% = Access to Healthcare

What We Spend on Being Healthy?

88% = Medical Services

4% = Healthful Behaviors

8% = Other[36]

These percentages present a staggering opportunity. In Solie's words, "the central challenge of aging is not access to healthcare, which is certainly important. Rather, it is the search for and access to strategies that help us mobilize and sustain healthful behaviors. In this regard, it is the holy grail of aging."[37]

When the Fidelity study was published, it was pointed out that "[t]he biggest return on investment for retirement comes from healthful lifestyle choices now. Controlling weight, exercising, eating nutritious foods will for the vast majority of people significantly lower their health care costs in the future … If wise personal health choices were adopted widely, health insurance premiums and Medicare expenses would ultimately decrease as well."[38]

It's estimated that for approximately the next 20 years, 10,000 baby boomers will retire *every single day*. At that rate, one in five Americans will be retired by 2030.[39] Furthermore, with our increased knowledge of healthful lifestyle choices like eating well and exercising and the startling improvements in medical technology, 50% of children born since 2000 will live to

---

36 David Solie, *How to Say It to Seniors: Closing the Communication Gap with Our Elders*, (Upper Saddle River, NJ: Prentice Hall Press, 2004).

37 *Ibid*.

38 BK, North Carolina, letter commenting on "New Estimate Sees Rise in Medical Costs in Retirement," *The New York Times*, May 9, 2012

39 James Crabtree, "Agnes the Aging Suit," *FT Magazine*, July 22, 2011

100.[40] As time goes by, a whole lot more people will be in their retirement years. All these factors will contribute to the continuing rise in medical costs.

Fortunately, both you and your aging parents can work toward mitigating your healthcare costs. It's all a matter of changing certain lifestyle habits. Not only will you feel better and enjoy life more, but your improved health will also mean fewer trips to the doctor. And fewer trips to the doctor leads to less of your money spent on co-pays, deductibles, and prescription medicine. An all-around good deal.

The major chronic killers of today are heart disease, strokes, cancer, and diabetes. Yet the odds of being stricken by any of these can be lowered through healthful eating and exercise. We can choose to lower our risks and have fun in the process.

According to the Centers for Disease Control and Prevention (CDC), 40% of deaths in America today are due to smoking, lack of exercise, eating unhealthful foods, and alcohol abuse.[41] Nearly half the deaths today could be delayed. Life could be enhanced by simply taking the time to look after oneself. Good news, indeed!

Let's see if we've got this right. If we eat better, healthful food that tastes great, and we get out and participate in fun activities that will connect us with people we love and introduce us to new people to meet, we'll spend less money on healthcare and live longer? Seems like a no-brainer to me.

The rest of this section will look at the specific steps we can take to make this concept a reality. But first, how do we broach the subject of changing a lifetime's set of health habits with our parents and loved ones?

---

40 S. Jay Olshansky and Bruce A. Carnes, "Ageing and Health," The Lancet, January 2, 2010, http://www.thelancet.com/journals/lancet/article/PIIS0140-6736(09)62177-2/fulltext

41 Arthur Schoenstadt, MD, *Senior Healthy Living - A Guide to Living a Healthy Lifestyle*, September 19, 2007, http://www.senior-health.emedtv.com

Having the Health Talk

As with each aspect of the talk, the best way to begin the health talk is to imagine yourself in your parents' shoes. To quote David Solie again, "[i]n almost every conversation with an older adult, control and legacy issues rise to the surface.... Once we understand this gap and begin to appreciate it, the clash fades away. How? Because we stop fighting our elders for the one thing they will not surrender: the control they need to manage their lives and shape their legacies."[42]

So, begin by understanding what motivates your parents, and don't push against them here. Although they're worried about retaining what control they have while garnering meaning out of their lives, switching to tofu and joining the local yoga center may not be at the top of their to-do list. Bustling in and telling them to throw out the store-bought muffins and join the local gym may be met with a polite nod, but nothing long-lasting will come of it.

A much better avenue is to emphasize how, through eating healthier and exercising more, they'll have *more* control over their lives because they'll feel better and live longer. They'll be able to spend more quality time with their family doing the things they love to do and spend less time worrying about when they'll have to give up important things that keep them independent and mobile like driving. Increasing their healthful choices will actually help them with their motivators. How beautiful is that?

As always, pick the right time and setting to begin talking about healthful lifestyle choices. This can be neatly combined with the financial discus-

---

42   Solie, *How to Say It to Seniors*, Op. cit., p. 21

sion because they're a natural fit. When you and your parents understand the huge cost ramifications of poor health (as stated in the Fidelity study), it makes emphasizing things like going for more walks a natural.

But improving health isn't just a financial matter. Your parents can live longer and happier, too. Life is more fun when you feel good. And the more fun it is, the more you want to do. It's a pleasant cycle, indeed.

What to Discuss

To start the talk, consider discussing issues that are listed on the following checklist. This will lead into areas of importance specific to your family's situation.

Ask the following:

- Do you have regular physical checkups?
- Do you participate in any exercise programs?
- Which family member, if any, is aware of any health conditions that could impact your situation either now or in the future?
- Do you have an updated list of all medications taken and is someone aware of this?
- What family member or close friend knows of any existing medical conditions and their treatment?
- Have you made absolutely clear to anyone of your end-of-life wishes? This includes when and if they should terminate life support and potential living arrangements in the case of tragedy or poor health?
- Do you have much stress in your life? If so, do you have a plan for eliminating it?
- How have you evaluated your health plan options?

Through the answers to these questions, you can ascertain potential problem areas, as well as open up the conversation to healthful lifestyle choices. As always, consider using anecdotes of friends or other family members to illustrate your point.

Did Aunt Mary die from diabetes she could have prevented? Did your best friend's widower father stop smoking, start running, and just complete his first marathon, and, in the process, lost 40 pounds and met his future wife?

Show them through personal stories how Aunt Mary lost control of her life through ill health, and your best friend's father took a new lease on life because of his healthful habits. These points will appeal to their core motivators of keeping control and maintaining a legacy.

Taking Ownership

A critical point for you to remember is these are your parent's lifestyle choices, not yours. Think back to the statistics above from the Bipartisan Policy Center. Fifty percent of our health is related to behavioral choices. If we add a healthful environment, that means 70% of our health is in our control. Only 20% is in our genes and 10% is a result of access to healthcare. But, that 70% is 100% their decision. Your job is to show them what life can look like as a healthy retiree. Add to this those concrete steps they can take to achieve that life. Their job is to take action, and they must make the choice to do so.

Gordon Filepas is the author of the brilliant book *Lean and Healthy to 100*. He lists seven steps to living a healthy and long life. For more detailed information, get his book, but for the purposes of this section, it's relevant to note his very first step: Accept personal responsibility.

Your healthful choices and those of your parents', are just that: choices. What you can do though is help educate yourself and your parents so everyone knows which are the best choices to make.

Filepas goes on to describe the benefits of healthful eating, regular exercise, and getting plenty of sleep. He even emphasizes the importance of relieving emotional baggage and stress. After all, our bodies and minds are linked in ways that science is proving are deeper than ever before realized.

Making healthful choices isn't that difficult and the benefits are enormous. But first, your parents must decide for themselves to take responsibility for their healthful choices. You can certainly lead them in the right direction, though. And remember, you can apply everything you learn here, too. It's never too soon to start making healthful choices and feeling better.

Smoking

One immediate place to begin making healthful choices is if you or your parents smoke. You know what I'm going to say next: Quit!

"But it's not that easy," you reply.

I know. But nowadays your doctor can help with nicotine reducing drugs and stop-smoking programs. Tobacco use, which includes smoking and dipping, is the single most preventable cause of death in the United States. Nearly half a million people die each year from tobacco-related diseases. One in five deaths are due to smoking and nearly 50,000 of those are from secondhand smoke.[43]

Quitting smoking is an excellent choice to make.

If someone you love smokes (that includes yourself), encourage him or her to see a doctor about ways to stop. Each time a cigarette is lit up, that person is unnecessarily a little bit closer to death. Consider it this way: If you smoke and don't mind dramatically increasing the risk of dying prematurely, think about your loved ones instead. They don't want to lose you. Each time you light up, you hurt them as much as you hurt yourself.

Make the choice to quit and then do the following:

- See your doctor for medicines and programs to help.
- Set a specific date to quit.
- Tell your friends and family. Ask for their support. They'll love you for it.
- Join a quit-smoking support group.
- If you slip up and have a cigarette after you quit, don't beat yourself up. Just start again. Many times it takes more than one try to be successful.

---

[43] Centers for Disease Control, http://www.cdc.gov/tobacco/data_statistics/fact_sheets/health_effects/tobacco_related_mortality/

- Don't let yourself have "just one puff."

I remember when my sister and I sat our mom down when we were in our late teens. We all sat at the dining room table and we asked our mom, who had been smoking since her teens—it was thought to be cool even back then—to quit smoking. She looked at my father, who didn't smoke and didn't say a word, and then she looked at us. With tears in her eyes, she said, "Okay," and she never smoked a cigarette again.

It is possible for anyone at any age to quit smoking, and you or any one else in your family can be the person to help your parents to do it.

14

Exercise:
Living Healthier Step-by-Step

A recent report by the medical journal *The Lancet*[44] estimated that 9% of deaths worldwide—that's more than 5.3 million people in 2008—were due to a lack of physical activity. This puts it at the same level of mortality as for smokers.

The report stated that "[s]trong evidence shows that physical inactivity increases the risk of many adverse health conditions, including major non-communicable diseases such as coronary heart disease, type 2 diabetes, and breast and colon cancers, and shortens life expectancy. Because much of the world's population is inactive, this link presents a major public health issue."[45]

This is no mild warning for couch potatoes to get up and go shopping. The report proves a strong and deadly link between sitting on our hind ends too much and premature death.

Exercise also improves memory and cognitive function and reduces the chances of dementia and depression. One study found that for women aged 65 and older, each extra mile walked per week reduced the chance of cognitive decline by 13%.[46]

---

44 http://www.lancet.com/journals/lancet/article/PIIS0140-6736(12)61031-9/fulltext
45 Dr. I-Min Lee, ScD, et al., "Effect of physical inactivity on major non-communicable diseases worldwide: an analysis of burden of disease and life expectancy," *The Lancet*, Vol. 380, Issue 9838, pp. 219-229, 21 July 2012
46 Cameron L. Martz, ACSM H/FI, *Healthy Living for Seniors*, http://www.divefitness.com

However, according to researchers at Penn State and the University of Maryland, Americans get on average only 17 minutes of exercise a day (119 minutes a week).[47] A Statistics Canada study published in 2011 found only 15% of Canadians meet the recommended 150 minutes of physical activity each week.[48]

Compare this with data from the Nielson Company showing that in 2010, Americans watched on average *35 hours* a week of television.[49] That's nearly the same as we spend at a fulltime job! Yet, we don't have "time" to get enough exercise. Something's wrong with this picture.

Given this shocking data, it's easy to see one ginormous place where our efforts on improving healthful lifestyles need to be. We need to put down the potato chips, turn off the TV, and go for a walk or workout.

So how much exercise should we be getting and what type should it be? The CDC gives the following guidelines for adults:[50]

- Two and a half hours (150 minutes) of moderate-intensity aerobic exercise a week, *and* muscle strengthening activities two days a week. The latter should work every major muscle group: legs, hips, back, abdomen, chest, and arms.
- Or, one hour and fifteen minutes (75 minutes) of vigorous exercise per week, and the above two days of muscle strengthening.
- Or, an equal mix of moderate to vigorous activity per week along with two days of strength training.

The CDC emphasizes it's just fine to break your 150 minutes of exercise up into smaller amounts. The minimum chunk of time that counts is ten minutes. That sounds pretty doable!

---

47 Sylvia Booth Hubbard, *Average American Gets 17 Minutes of Exercise a Day,* May 9, 2012, http://www. newsmaxhealth.com
48 Carly Weeks, "Do You Get 150 Minutes of Exercise Each Week? Here's Why You Should," *The Globe and Mail,* July 22, 2012
49 Brian Stelter, "TV Viewing Continues to Edge Up," *The New York Times,* January 2, 2011
50 Centers for Disease Control and Prevention, "How much physical activity do adults need?" http://www.cdc.gov/physicalactivity/everyone/guidelines/adults.html

Their Web site also states that if you increase the amount of activity you do, your health benefits will also increase. So think of the above as minimums and try to gradually do better.

One way to get your parents started on this can be to enlist a friend who likes to walk or exercise, or even join them on a short scenic nature walk. Bring along a grandchild to make it even more compelling.

<u>Living Well, Not Just Longer</u>

Although it's a well-known fact that people on average are living longer, I frequently hear a comment similar to, "Why would I want to live longer when my back hurts, my legs ache, I have to take all these pills, and I can't remember a thing? What's in it for me!"

An interesting point, indeed! Americans are living longer, but this also coincides with more heart disease, cancer, and other chronic diseases that are, plain and simple, no fun to live with. Researchers have actually given it a name: "lengthening of morbidity." In other words, we've extended our lives, but as a result, also the amount of time we may spend dealing with chronic disease.

However, it isn't all bleak and bleary. A new study published by the Archives of Internal Medicine[51] found that physical fitness affects *how* you age, too. Specifically, they assessed the aerobic fitness of over 18,000 men and women at the age of 49. They classified these people into five fitness-level groups, then reassessed their health when they were in their 70s and 80s. The results were astounding.

Researchers at the University of Texas Southwestern Medical Center and the Cooper Institute in Dallas found that those people least fit when they were 49 (unfortunately, the majority of the participants), were most likely to suffer from chronic disease such as cancer, heart disease, Alzheimer's, and diabetes later in life.

On the other hand, and this is where the good news comes in, "the most aerobically fit people lived with chronic illnesses in the final five years of

---

51 Gretchen Reynolds, "The Benefits of Middle-Age Fitness," *The New York Times*, September 5, 2012

their lives, instead of the final 10, 15, or even 20 years." The participants didn't necessarily live longer, but they certainly lived better on average.

This is a startling case for getting and staying fit as soon as possible. It doesn't mean you need to become a triathlete. All it takes is 20-30 minutes of light aerobic exercise most days of the week. Every single one of us can manage that. It boils down to developing and maintaining good habits.

Some of our physical well-being is attributable to genetics, but not all of it. Looking after ourselves by exercising and eating right plays an enormous role.

What Counts as "Exercise"?

The CDC states that moderate aerobic activity is when you're still able to talk while you're exercising, but not able to sing. Vigorous activity would be when you can say just a few words at a time and then need to catch your breath again.

Many ways exist to get your weight training, and it doesn't have to just be in that stinky ol' gym. Lifting weights is great, but so is working with resistance bands, doing resistance exercises such as sit-ups and pushups, heavy gardening, and yoga.

Beginning an exercise program can also be a great way people can make the routines of their work life (waking up, getting dressed, and going to work) part of their retirement life. Keeping similar hours and routines can be a way to transition into retirement. Including exercise into those routines will make for an even better retirement.

Walking

Let's look at some of the myriad ways that exist to make exercise something your parents will wake up looking forward to doing. For some of us, the idea of trudging off to the gym or for a painful run is off putting at best, even though gym use and running are both excellent ways to get exercise.

The American Association of Retired People (AARP) says that walking might just be the most practical and enjoyable form of exercise for many people.[52] The good news? Provided you keep up a brisk pace, walking 150

---

52   Candy Sagon, "Walking: The Easiest Exercise," AARP Web site, December 21, 2011, http://www.aarp.org/health/healthy-living/info-12-2011/walking-health-benefits.html

minutes a week completely satisfies the CDC's recommended minimum exercise per week.

Suggest to your parents that they make walking a daily habit in a variety of ways. Can they walk to work? Walk to their friend's house? How about walking to the store when they need only a couple of items? Many retired people walk circuits at the local mall, which helps when the weather's bad. Or they could simply find a nice park and discover it on foot.

Rick Genter was obese at 400 pounds, yet he was only 51. In his words, "My whole family is obese. My mother died at the age of 56. My father is at least 150 pounds overweight and on all sorts of medication. I had high cholesterol, high triglycerides, and I was convinced I was on my way to diabetes, a heart attack, or both."[53]

Rick decided to take control of his health and life and began an exercise program of, you guessed it, walking. He began with 30 minutes on his lunch break and found he loved it. As he started to lose weight, the walking became easier, and he was motivated to walk even more. He finished up walking seven miles to and from work each day, lost 200 pounds, and recently got married. Now that's a success story.

Here are tips from the AARP for getting started on a walking program.[54]

- Start slowly. Ten minutes at a time is fine. Then slowly build up.
- Break your goal into chunks. Three ten-minute walks count as 30 minutes for the day.
- Get a good, comfortable pair of walking shoes.
- Keep a daily log. It helps you to see the progress you're making.

Other walking activities could be

- Walk when playing golf.
- Join a walking group. Check with your local gym or community center.
- If you have grandkids, take them for a walk somewhere fun, like the zoo, a park, or an amusement center.

---

53 Ibid.
54 Ibid.

- Walk to lunch with a friend.
- Find a "walking partner." You can keep each other motivated and on a schedule.
- Walk in the mall on bad weather days.
- Don't turn on the TV until you've done your 30 minutes of walking.
- Take the stairs everywhere you can.
- Get an iPod and listen to music or books while you walk so that it's something that you can do on your own.

These simple lifestyle changes can actually add years onto your life, years when you'll feel good and are full of energy and high-spirited. Start slowly and see where it takes you.

More Fitness Activities

Walking more can become part of everyone's lifestyle changes. But you and your parents' exercise programs don't have to end there. If you're out of shape, walking is a great way to gradually get back into the swing of being active. For most people, they'll find that the better they feel, the more they want to do.

Some of our routine activities can be turned into productive exercise events. You might be amazed at what you can turn into "fitness."

Consider the following:

- Housecleaning. Yes, if you hop to it, your heartrate will rise during vacuuming, dusting, and scrubbing.
- Rake leaves and other physical gardening work.
- Join your community center and take classes in dancing. This is a great way to meet people too.
- Yoga. Many forms exist, so make sure yours gets your heartrate up. Done properly, yoga counts as both cardiovascular and muscle training. Studies have shown people simply feel better when they include yoga in their regular weekly routine.

- Take up a new sport, like tennis, biking, swimming, or hiking. Clubs and groups may exist for each of these to help you get started and motivated.
- Sex. Yes, remember any activity that gets your heartrate going counts as exercise.
- Watch exercise shows on TV, or on tapes and CDs.
- Join a gym!
- Hire a personal trainer to set you up with a training program you can do on your own.
- Teach your grandkids a sport, like golfing or tennis. If you're golfing, make sure you walk as much as possible.
- Wear a pedometer to see how many steps you take each day. Work on increasing this number. But remember, you need to do ten continuous minutes of exercise for it to count toward your daily and weekly goals.

Encourage your parents to keep a fitness log. This way they'll know how much they're doing and can watch themselves improve. This is great for motivation. If you don't know how many minutes you're exercising each week, then you won't know how much to increase or vary. Be sure to talk to them about getting enough rest, too. Sleep works wonders for our bodies and minds. Try to get six to eight hours of good quality sleep each night. Siestas (that sounds so much better than naps) are great, too. Keep them short—20 minutes is a good target[55]. They're a wonderful way to revitalize midday.

Exercise doesn't have to be painful and boring. When approached as a way of life, rather than a torturous set of hours each week, your parents will enjoy it more and reap more of the benefits.

We want to live longer, of course, but we also want those years to be filled with positive memories and events. Being physically healthy is an essential part of the picture. Life's more fun when you feel good.

---

55 http://ririanproject.com/2007/09/05/10-benefits-of-power-napping-and-how-to-do-it/

15

Eating Your Way to Good Health

A healthful diet is important throughout life, but as we age, it becomes even more so. Good nutrition leads to a higher resistance to disease and illnesses, faster recuperation times if we do fall ill, and overall higher energy levels and positive outlooks.

Eating well, just as increasing our level of physical fitness, can save us money. The USDA estimates that healthier diets could save $71 billion in health related costs. This figure isn't surprising given that the CDC estimates that 61% of Americans are "seriously overweight or obese."[56]

Fortunately, eating nutritious, delicious food fits right in with our new awareness of the importance of exercise. What better way to reward yourself for that workout or extra long walk than to enjoy a meal your body will love, too.

Heart disease and strokes, high blood pressure, obesity, cancer, bone loss, and type 2 diabetes can all be prevented or brought under control with a healthy diet,[57] especially in combination with a fitness regimen. The immune system is boosted, and muscles, organs, and other body parts are kept in better shape to keep you healthy.

---

56   "Why good nutrition is important," Center for Science in the Public Interest, http://www.cspinet.org/nutritionpolicy/nutrition_policy.html; http://www.cdc.gov/obesity/data/adult.html
57   Jeanne Segal, Ph.D., and Gina Kemp, M.A., "Senior nutrition: Feeding the mind, body, and soul," June 2012, http://www.helpguide.org

As well, certain vitamins and other nutrients keep the mind sharper, the memory better, and help ward off dementia. To top it all off, healthy food simply makes you feel and look better. Now who can argue with that?

It turns out that the saying "you are what you eat" is surprisingly true.

The Senior Metabolism

No surprise to some, aging takes many forms. Our metabolism change, as do our senses, digestion, and mental well-being. By better understanding some of these changes, we can find better, tasty solutions.

Helpguide.org, a nonprofit organization devoted to educating people on health and family issues, points out six areas to be aware of:[58]

1) A slowing metabolism. Anybody who just can't shed those last few pounds knows what I mean. We burn fewer calories and tend to be less active. (That won't be the case once you've added exercise to your and your parents' lifestyles!)

2) Weakening senses. Our ability to taste and smell decreases as we age. We may find ourselves salting our foods more just to get extra flavor out of them. Instead, by adding spices and natural flavors to our foods, this is easily overcome.

3) More medications. Some medications can increase or decrease our appetites, and others reduce our sense of taste. If you think this is your or your parents' case, see your doctor as to which drug it might be and find alternative options.

4) A slowing digestive system. Less saliva and stomach acid are produced as we age, so it can be more difficult for our bodies to digest not only foods, but also vitamins and minerals. Ways to counteract this are to eat more fiber and take vitamin and mineral supplements.

5) Loneliness and depression. These can lead to either increased or decreased appetites. I'll cover more on these issues in the next section, "Keeping a Positive Attitude."

---

58 *Ibid.*

6) Widows and widowers. Sometimes people on their own just don't have the get up and go to fix proper meals. Again, the next two sections will cover mental health and staying active, both excellent solutions for numbers 5 and 6.

Understanding the problem is, in itself, half the solution. By recognizing the metamorphoses you and your parents will be going through, the solutions will more easily follow.

A Healthful Diet vs. Dieting

It's important to make a distinction between having a healthful diet and dieting. The two have very different goals.

Dieting refers to restricting the calories you take in with the end goal of losing weight. Done properly, dieting is effective. Done improperly, dieting can injure your health by lowering your immune system, reducing your muscle tissue and bone density, depleting your energy, and, most of the time, gaining the weight back you've worked so hard to lose.

Having a healthful diet, on the other hand, is different. A healthful diet refers to eating foods rich in nutrients and vitamins, and low in saturated fats, chemicals, sugar, and preservatives. With a healthful diet we feel better, our bodies function better, we are more resistant to illness and disease, and, over time, we achieve our natural weight. In conjunction with an exercise program, healthful eating extends the quality and longevity of our life.

The Talk and Healthy Eating

For many of us, our eating habits have been carved into our lifestyles over decades. Don't expect to sit down with your parents, hand them a sparkling new list of foods to eat and avoid, and expect them to abide by your instructions. They'll more likely pat you on the hand, say, "That's interesting, sweetie," and go on eating what they've always eaten.

Permanent change best comes gradually and through education. Help your parents understand why they need to make changes in their diet and what the benefit for them will be. Remember to emphasize that when they feel good and are healthy, they'll be in more control of their lives. This is what's most important.

Gradually, introduce them to new ways of eating. Take trips together to farmers markets. Emphasize organic food and how much better it tastes. Take along the grandkids and make it a family outing. Go shopping with your parents and help them learn to make healthful choices. Be sure to explain why, but don't lecture them. No one likes a know-it-all. Let them take part. Your role is that of a guide.

Holiday meals can be a huge source of bad fats, sugars, and unnecessary calories. Set the example by preparing healthful holiday meals, and show your parents how they taste great. You can really impress them by you ability to incorporate family traditions and rituals into a healthful holiday meal (it's a good challenge to make for yourself).

Many people of older generations were raised on "meat and potatoes." Hence, these are normal foods for them. The key here is to get your parents to agree to try new foods. They need to take responsibility for eating better. Go slowly and let them gradually learn that "healthy" doesn't have to mean "tastes like cardboard."

Ask them to include a new fruit or vegetable at every meal. And by vegetable, I mean fresh, colorful, and, ideally, raw or lightly cooked. Teach them to add spices and healthy fat, if any, like a quality olive oil. Get them into the habit of a small side salad at every meal. This is a great way to get more nutrients and fiber. If they're in the habit of eating deserts, start out by asking them to eat half as much. Then gradually substitute yogurt and fruit or other healthful alternatives.

Finally, try to get your parents to think about how they feel after a healthful meal. Are they less bloated and do they have more energy? Are they interested in having an after-dinner walk rather than watching TV?

Some folks catch on quickly to healthful diets; others take more time. Either way, with gentle gradual coaching and setting a positive example yourself, you can change your parents' lives for the better through what they eat.

How Many Calories?

First off, many health experts say the days of counting calories are over. With a healthful eating and exercise regimen, your body will find its natural weight. However, some of us still want to know what's the correct amount of calories we should be eating every day.

The National Institute on Aging provides the following guidelines:

For women over the age of fifty:

- 1,600 calories a day if you're not physically active,
- 1,800 calories a day if you're somewhat active, and
- 2,000 calories a day if you're very active.

For men over the age of fifty:

- 2,000 calories a day if you're not physically active,
- 2,200-2,400 calories a day if you're somewhat active, and
- 2,400-2,800 calories a day if you're very active.

Many books and Web sites exist where you can find out how many calories each food has. But remember, calories are just one piece of the overall equation and come from our days of "dieting." What's more important is that you and your parents eat fresh, preferably organic, vegetables and fruits, fish, nuts, and whole grains. But I'll get more into that in just a minute.

Malnutrition

Unfortunately, even in this Age of Obesity, malnutrition is a problem for some seniors. Perhaps you've seen elderly people who are much too thin and look as if a strong wind would snap them in half. Malnutrition is caused by not eating enough; however, this can be caused by digestive problems. Food isn't being assimilated properly, and the calories and nutrients aren't utilized. Prescription meds can have the adverse side effect of loss of appetite, as can depression. And any combination of these issues can exist, too.

The side effects of malnutrition are terrible: weakened immune systems, depression, fatigue, lung and heart problems, and even poor skin.[59]

If you think one or both of your parents are suffering from malnutrition, consider the following:

- See a doctor to determine the cause.
- Encourage them to eat high-calorie foods.
- Get them to snack.
- Encourage them to eat with other people.
- Hire Meals on Wheels or organize some other help in preparing food.
- If you think depression is the cause, then seek help from your doctor as to how to combat this issue.

So, What's in a Healthful Diet?

Recent studies have shown that not all calories are alike; hence, my disclaimer in the previous chapter on calories. The New Balance Foundation Obesity Prevention Center of Boston's Children's Hospital recently analyzed not only what works to help people lose weight, but more importantly, also what helps them keep that weight off.[60]

In a nutshell, eating 100 calories worth of sugar-laden gummy bears is not the same as 100 calories worth of fresh spinach. Although it seems kind of like common sense, the proof is now coming in.

The study looked at three common diets:

- A standard low fat diet, with calories coming from 60% carbohydrates, 20% protein, and 20% fat.
- An ultra-low fat diet, much like the Atkins, with 10% carbohydrates, 60% fat, and 30% protein.

---

59 Jeanne Segal, Ph.D., and Gina Kemp, M.A., "Understanding malnutrition," June 2012, http://www.helpguide.org
60 Mark Bittman, "Which Diet Works?" *The New York Times*, June 26, 2012

- A low-glycemic diet, with 40% carbohydrates (consisting of minimally processed grains, fruit, vegetables, and beans—this is important), 40% fat, and 20% protein.

The "glycemic" level of food refers to the measure of glucose (blood sugar) increase from consuming carbohydrates. Not all carbohydrates behave the same. Carbohydrates that break down easily and quickly in the digestive system increase the amount of sugar in the blood quickly. These are high on the "glycemic index" (GI). Examples of these foods would be simple carbohydrates like white breads, sugar, white rice, and potatoes.

Low-glycemic index food releases more slowly and stably into the blood stream. Examples of these foods would be fruits and vegetables, legumes (beans), nuts, and some whole unprocessed grains.

So the 40% of carbohydrates referred to in the third diet studied (the low-glycemic diet) would be carbs with a low GI (glycemic index).

The results of the study were fascinating. The folks on the ultra low-carb diet (Atkins equivalent) actually burned 350 *more* calories than those on the traditional low-fat diet when both consumed the same amount of calories. Those on the low GI diet burned 150 more calories than the traditional low-fat diet. Remember, the traditional low-fat diet has been shown to affect our insulin resistance (a factor in diabetes) and to lower our good cholesterol (HDL). It's not a healthy alternative.

So, it would seem that the Atkins style diet is the way to go. You actually burn more calories than the other two.

However (there's always a "however," isn't there?), the Atkins diet showed other health-related issues that one would want to avoid. Specifically, the Atkins increased inflammation, and reduced cortisol, which helps us deal with stress. Stress is one of the primary killers of all. This mixture increased the chances for long-term heart risk.

The message for us? The low GI diet is the best combination overall. It's a healthier choice than either the low-fat or low-carb alternatives, and is actually quite good for us.

The director of the center that performed the study, David Ludwig, said it this way: "It's time to reacquaint ourselves with minimally processed carbs. If you take three servings of refined carbohydrates (white bread, potatoes, white rice, etc.) and substitute one for fruit, one of beans, and one of nuts, you could eliminate 50% of diet-related disease in the United States."[61]

Wow!

Let's look more closely at what a low GI way of eating consists of. The good news is a lot of it is common sense as to what's healthy for you.

"Good" carbohydrates. As I mentioned, these include fruits and vegetables, nuts, legumes, and whole unprocessed grains. Many good sources of information exist to help you understand which carbs have a low GI.[62]

"Good" fats. The low GI way of eating recommends 40% good fats. Thinking of eating fat can be off putting, but we actually need good fats in our diet on a regular basis. They have great vitamins, provide essential fatty acids, and make our skin look wonderful.

Let's look at good versus bad fats.

Good fats are unsaturated, both monounsaturated and polyunsaturated fats. We get these in:

- good oils like, olive, sunflower, canola, peanut, and sesame oils
- avocados
- olives
- nuts
- fatty fish like salmon, tuna, mackerel, herring, and trout
- tofu

Bad fats, on the other hand, we want to avoid. They're called saturated and trans fats, and occur in:

- fatty cuts of meat as in beef, lamb, and pork, and in chicken with the skin

---

61 *Ibid.*
62 http://www.health.harvard.edu/newsweek/Glycemic_index_and_glycemic_load_for_100_foods.htm

- whole fat dairy products, like milk, cheese, cream, butter, and ice cream
- lard
- most pastries, cookies, cakes, muffins and pizza dough (it is possible to make healthy varieties of all of these)
- packaged snack foods like potato chips, microwave popcorn, and crackers
- margarine
- fried foods, such as French fries and fried chicken and fish
- candy bars

If you think about it, there aren't many surprises in the above lists. It's just a matter of making the healthful, common sense choices. Once you get started, the "bad" fat foods just won't taste as good. Your body adjusts surprisingly quickly to healthful foods.

"Good" proteins. It logically follows that good proteins will be low in bad fats. Consider eating chicken without the skin, fatty fish as listed above (they're full of good fat), low-fat yogurt and cheese, eggs, and beans. Lean beef and pork can occasionally be added to the mix.

In other words, eat a diet of fresh fruits, vegetables, unprocessed whole grains, avocados, olives, nuts, lean meat, fatty fish, eggs, and low-fat yogurt and cheese. In fact, this way of eating is like taking a step back in time. Many people in the Mediterranean still eat this way naturally.

The Most Important Meal of the Day

Your mother was right. Breakfast is the most important meal, but I don't mean a breakfast of fried eggs and bacon with white toast and butter. Breakfast is the first meal after a long period without any food and provides energy for your body. Thus, the name "break-fast"; you break the food "fast" you were on while you slept (and you didn't think you were doing anything productive while you slept).

That first meal of the day sets you and your body off on the right foot for the rest of the day. Studies have shown that, "regular breakfast eaters over their lifetime stay in a healthier weight range than people who are hit or miss, or those who regularly skip breakfast."[63]

The key is to skip the sweet muffin and cereals and, instead, make sure you get enough protein. If you start the day on a sugar high, you'll find that your energy won't last. By midafternoon you'll be low on energy, may have mood swings, and will be looking for a pick-me-up in the form of food or caffeine.

Instead, protein in the form of eggs, nuts, or fatty fish like salmon, (all low GI) will give your body stamina and energy until the next normal mealtime. You can balance out this protein with fresh fruit and whole grains (think oatmeal).

Watch out for boxed cereal and store bought granola bars. Both these are often sold as "healthy alternatives," but read the fine print. Many are chock full of sugar, refined grains, and preservatives. One children's cereal, Kellogg's Honey Snacks, contains 56% sugar by weight.[64]

So read the labels carefully. Look for low sugar (less than 8 grams per serving) and high fiber (at least 4 grams per serving). This is the magic formula. Even then, eat a small bowl and supplement with fruit and low-fat yogurt and/or nuts.

The Problem with Dairy

Most of have been raised thinking that drinking a glass of milk is good for us, even long after we're no longer children. The American Dairy Association (which is a powerful lobbying group) suggests that we drink four 8-ounce glasses of milk a day. That's one whole quart of milk a day![65]

Problems abound with this guideline. First, up to 50 million Americans are lactose intolerant (including yours truly): 90% of Asians, and 75% of Af-

---

63 Lena Sin, "Breakfast dos and don'ts to get your body off to a healthy start every day," *The Province*, July 22, 2012
64 *Ibid.*
65 Mark Bittman, "Got Milk? You Don't Need It," *The New York Times*, July 7, 2012

rican-Americans, Mexicans, and Jews. Approximately 1.3 million children are allergic to milk, making it the second most common food allergy after peanuts.

Mark Bittman, food guru, cookbook author, and *New York Times* columnist, had an "incurable" chronic upset stomach his entire life. This morphed into chronic heartburn or acid reflex. Over a considerable amount of years he tried all sorts of cures, but nothing worked. Then, one day, he decided to give up all dairy products. Twenty-four hours later his heartburn was gone, never to return.[66]

This is very similar to what happened to me. Since a child, I believed in the value and benefits of milk and drank my fill. As I got older and found a pack of Rolaids or Tums becoming a frequent companion in my pocket or on my night table, I started to wonder what caused my constant indigestion? I loved pizza and cookies with milk. I complained to my wife that no matter what I ate, I would get stomach discomfort. When she recommended that I try soy milk rather than regular milk for a week, it was like a revelation! I was cured.

These stories are staggering in what they teach and the opportunities they lay before us. Not only is it surprisingly common to have some degree of lactose intolerance or allergy to dairy products, but they're also full of "bad" fat. Dairy consumption has also been linked to Type 1 diabetes and certain forms of cancer. Yikes!

Sometimes people worry about the extra calcium dairy provides, and they would miss out on this important mineral. Yet studies have shown that the best way to gain and maintain bone strength is to exercise and take vitamin D.[67]

What does this all mean for you and your parents? Do what Mark Bittman and I did, give up dairy for five days and see how you feel. Instead, use soy or other lactose free products. If you feel fine after the five days, great, but still consider using dairy wisely and less frequently. Stick to low fat but make sure no sugar has been added to make up for less fat. Treat yourself

---

66 Ibid.
67 Ibid.

with a good, gooey cheese or small bowl of ice cream from time to time, but try to keep dairy consumption to a minimum.

Food and Eating Guidelines

Changing the way you and/or your parents eat doesn't need to be a painful ordeal. In fact, it can be fun. It's a matter of slowly changing bad habits into good ones and eating great food along the way.

But some tips and advice can be shared to make the journey easier. Have a look at these guidelines:

- Don't skip meals. This causes your metabolism to break its natural rhythm and can lead to bad choices later in the day.
- Snacking is okay. In fact, some food and diet gurus recommend five small meals a day, rather than three larger ones. If you do snack, make sure to stick to the low GI rule. Eat only vegetables, fruit, nuts, or another form of protein. Leave the chips and candy for a treat.
- Drink lots of water. This helps cleanse your system and breaks down fat into forms your muscles can use for fuel.
- Eat for color, too. Sounds strange, but color can signify a different form of nutrient, and we want as much variety as possible. So, make your meals colorful!
- Eat fruit, skip juices. Fruit contains fiber and helps slow the intake of sugar into the bloodstream. Juices, on the other hand, can be like an injection of sugar, as much of the breaking down process has been done for us.
- Take a quality multivitamin. Talk to your doctor about which are best and if there are any additional supplements you should be taking. You should also discuss with them the potential for adverse effects that specific vitamin supplements can have if you're also taking certain prescription medication.
- Eat organic when you can. You don't have to start your own vegetable garden (unless you want to), but steering clear of unhealthy and

unnecessary pesticides, fungicides, and herbicides is common sense. More and more evidence is pointing to the danger of chemicals in our food.

- Floss daily. Do what? That's right, regular flossing reduces inflammation in our bodies. Those who don't incorporate this simple activity into their daily routine have a higher risk of heart disease, diabetes, and osteoporosis. It's also good for your teeth.

- Ask your doctor about taking a baby aspirin every day. Studies are showing the numerous positive effects of this simple habit.

- Get adventurous. Try new recipes, eat those strange green vegetables you've never bought before, and cook something you've never tried. Have fun!

16

Your Brain as the Key to Longevity

Daniel Amen, M.D., is a clinical neurologist, psychiatrist, and brain-imaging expert. He's also the author of the fascinating book *Use Your Brain to Change Your Age; Secrets to Look, Feel, and Think Younger Every Day*.[68]

Amen's well-documented premise is that an unhealthy lifestyle ages our brains prematurely, while the opposite also holds true: A healthy lifestyle can mend aging brains and prolong the length and quality of our lives. If you think about it, our brains are the CPU of our entire bodies. Everything we do, consciously, subconsciously, and unconsciously, is managed and controlled by our brains. From our moods to our relationships to how quickly we walk and how far we run, our brains are in charge.

In Amen's words, "Even though your brain consists of only 2 percent of the body's weight, it uses 20-30 percent of the calories you consume. Of the breakfast you had this morning or the dinner you had tonight, approximately a quarter of it went to feed your brain. Your brain also consumes 20 percent of the oxygen and blood flow in the body and it never rests (even during sleep).... *Your brain is the most energy hungry and expensive real estate in your body.*"[69]

---

68   Daniel G. Amen, M.D., *Use Your Brain to Change Your Age; Secrets to Look, Feel, and Think Younger Every Day* (New York: Crown Publishing Group), 2012.
69   *Ibid.*, p. 11

Brain Risk Behavior

According to Amen, negative lifestyle behaviors damage this all-important central processing unit, and healthful behaviors increase its efficiency and, therefore, the quality of your life. For the full details I highly recommend you read Amen's book. However, here is a short-list of brain-negative behavior:

- unhealthy friends or a lack of an emotional support group; basically, the reality is that your friends affect your attitude, which effects your health
- toxins, such as drugs, excess alcohol, smoking, excess caffeine, and pollutants in the environment
- inflammation
- medical problems, such as heart disease, gum disease, diabetes, hypertension, low levels of omega-3 or vitamin D, and sleep apnea
- the standard American diet(!) of too much sugar and trans fats
- lack of exercise
- mental health issues
- lack of meaning and purpose in your life[70]

It all sounds kind of familiar, doesn't it? The very same behaviors I've been emphasizing (and will continue to do so in the following sections) are the ones that will make you and your parents brain-healthy, too. In short, it's not too late. Positive lifestyle changes make the brain function better, even with prior damage.

Brain Healthy Behavior

Amen goes on to list the 12 most important risk factors that we can actually change with our behavior. None of these will surprise you.

1) smoking
2) high blood pressure

---

70 *Ibid.*, pp. 13-16

3) overweight or obese

4) lack of exercise

5) high fasting blood sugar levels

6) high LDL (bad) cholesterol levels

7) alcohol abuse, cancer, heart disease and strokes

8) low omega-3 fatty acids

9) eating high levels of saturated fats

10) eating low levels of unsaturated fats

11) high salt intake

12) not eating lots of fruits and vegetables[71]

Pretty much just what you've been reading all along. These healthy lifestyle changes affect so many important areas of our bodies and minds, and, therefore, our overall well-being and aging process.

Alzheimer's and Other Dementias

More than five million Americans probably have Alzheimer's, and this number is expected to rise dramatically over the coming decades. It's estimated that by 2050, over 88 million Americans will have this disease, which would be one out of every five people.[72] These numbers are staggering and make Amen's premise that we can improve brain function through our behavior all the more relevant.

Dementia in its various forms, including Alzheimer's, is all the more devastating when we take into account the financial cost as well as the emotional toll of watching loved ones fade. Amen estimates that 15 percent of caregivers of people with Alzheimer's actually have it themselves![73]

---

71 *Ibid.*, pp. 47-48
72 http://www.alzfdn.org/AboutAlzheimers/statistics.html
73 Amen, *Use Your Brain to Change Your Age, op. cit.*, p. 51

Alzheimer's Risk Factors

Nearly 50 percent of those people 85 and older have or will get Alzheimer's. So, why the difference? Why do half of us not get this terrible disease? No one knows for sure. There's no holy grail of Alzheimer's knowledge that let's doctors see for sure who will and will not succumb to this awful disease.

What we do know for sure is that dementia, and Alzheimer's in particular, actually starts forming in the brain before any symptoms exist. A seemingly healthy, active, and cognizant 40 year old may have early brain aging that will lead to Alzheimer's.

Amen has a list of "the most common risk factors for Alzheimer's disease and early brain aging."[74] Let's look at his list. In his book he rates each of these according to their seriousness.

Remember, just because you may have several of these risk factors doesn't mean you'll definitely come down with Alzheimer's. Equally, you may have none of the factors and yet still get it. These are guidelines, so we know what to work on within our own lives to raise the odds in our favor.

- one or more family members with Alzheimer's or dementia
- family history of Down's syndrome
- one head injury with loss of consciousness, or several head injuries with no loss of consciousness
- alcohol or drug abuse, past or present
- depression diagnosed by a physician, either past or present
- heart disease, heart attack, or stroke
- high cholesterol or high blood pressure
- diabetes
- history of cancer and cancer treatment
- seizures in the past or present

---
74   *Ibid.*, p. 52

- limited exercise
- less than a high school education
- a job that doesn't require learning new information
- age (the closer you get to 85, the higher the risk)
- smoking for ten or more years
- has one or more APOEe4 gene (genes believed to be associated with Alzheimer's)[75]

Reducing Your Alzheimer's Risk

Needless to say, some of the above risk factors can be dealt with more easily than others. You can't change your age or the fact you've had cancer, but you can eat right and exercise. You can work to lower your blood pressure and cholesterol. You can quit smoking. You can get your blood sugar and weight under control.

Amen references mental health research done by Dr. Deborah Barnes at the San Francisco VA Medical Center. Barnes's findings are astounding: "More than half of all Alzheimer's disease cases could potentially be prevented through lifestyle changes and treatment, or prevention of chronic medical conditions."[76]

Of the over 88 million people estimated to have Alzheimer's by 2050, 40 million of those cases could be prevented or the effects mitigated. Those numbers should get everyone's attention.

Dr. Barnes's research found that the biggest *modifiable* risk factors (that is, those you can go out today and start changing) are the following:

- physical inactivity
- depression
- smoking
- midlife hypertension

---

75 Ibid., pp. 52-53
76 Ibid., pp. 58

- midlife obesity
- low education
- diabetes

Barnes figures this group of risk factors alone counts for 51% of Alzheimer's cases worldwide, and 54% of cases in the US.[77] These results have been presented in major medical conferences and publications.

The message is clear. Bad lifestyle habits promote premature aging of the brain. Good lifestyle habits not only slow brain aging, but may also prevent you from getting Alzheimer's.

If any of the above seven modifiable risk factors are yours or those of your loved ones, the time to start fixing them is today. Not tomorrow, and not next week. It's not rocket science; it's discipline. The results of which will positively affect your life and, therefore, those of the people who love you.

---

77 *Ibid.*, pp. 59

17

Your Medical Team

If all of these lifestyle changes/horror stories seem overwhelming, don't worry. You've been taking in a lot of information, some of which may seem to raise more problems than solutions. How, exactly, are you going to get your 65-year-old father to stop smoking? Your mom's 40 pounds overweight and has tried every diet on Earth but still can't lose a pound. How are you going to convince her that what you have to say is any better than her other failed plans? Maybe you've found some Alzheimer's risk factors in your own life. How are you going to find the time to work on eliminating them with all the other things you have going on?

The good news is you're not alone. You actually have an entire medical team working with you and your parents. Your doctors and nurses are all part of the team. When organized properly, this will save you an enormous amount of time and effort and lower the risk of making mistakes.

Getting Organized

The first thing that needs to be addressed is figuring out the exact health-care and medical situation for each person. This means sorting through the medications taken, the doctors visited, and the appointments scheduled or need scheduling.

Make sure your parents have an up-to-date list of every single medication they take, what it's for, and the prescribed dosage. This will need to be reviewed as changes are made, much like an annual review for a financial portfolio.

David Solie has an excellent chart on his Web site for doing just this.[78] Here he asks you to list the following for each prescription drug:

- name of medication
- who prescribed it (your parents may have several doctors)
- what's it prescribed for
- the dosage
- the frequency
- what time to take it and with or without food
- when you started taking it
- which pharmacy you buy it from

Clearly outline the above for each drug. Then update the lists as changes are made. This is an excellent resource for organizing medications.

As your parents age, the number of doctors and specialists they visit will increase. This can be overwhelming, especially if both your mother and father are alive. I've seen elderly couples have close to a dozen different medical professionals they're working with.

Again, Solie comes to the rescue. He supplies an awesome chart on his Web site for each medical professional or group.[79] The chart includes not only the name of each professional, what they're seen for, and contact details, but also covers what their attitude is like, how easy they are to reach, and their willingness to explain the issues. All this is hugely valuable information. Getting organized at this level is an essential part of understanding your team.

Make sure you keep this information in an easily accessible location and that other family members and/or close friends know their whereabouts.

I want to stress the importance of being a partner with your parents when it comes to monitoring their health and the medications they take. My mom was a registered nurse for over 40 years and worked as an emergency

---

78 http://www.davidsolie.com/blog/the-medication-census/
79 http://www.davidsolie.com/blog/the-good-fit-mind-map/

room nurse on the night shift for over 25 of those years. What she saw in her lifetime at that job was more than anyone needs or wants to see when it comes to people and their health and illnesses. She saw tragedies on a regular basis. She would also talk about the miracles she saw at work.

All of the other nurses and doctors she worked with loved her. When my sister or I had questions about our health or that of our children, we would call mom and always find the answer or be directed to a doctor who was "the best" in that area.

I tell you all this because my mom died of an illness that neither my sister nor I were aware she had. This was not due to lack of communication—my sister spoke to my mom daily and I was a regular caller and visitor. When we cleaned out her house, we found medications that told the story of a woman in pain and illness. Needless to say we were devastated. The pain of not recognizing this haunts me to this day.

I assumed that my mom, being a health professional, was on top of her health and would share her medical situation and medications with us. If we had required she do that, would it have helped? Would we have been able to recognize that our mom had been hiding a cancer and her medical condition from us? Should we have been more diligent in tracking her health situation after my dad's recent death six months earlier?

How about the doctor?

Let's just say that you need to become more involved with your parents' health situations so that friendships and promises between a patient and their doctor don't hinder your ability to be fully aware of your parents' health.

This book and my previous one were written to help others to address the lessons that I learned from the tragedies of my mom and dad. Being an active partner with your parents in their relationships with their doctors and their medication situation can be the key to ensuring that what happened to my family doesn't happen to you.

Record the information I outlined using a pencil and paper or use the charts supplied by Solie on his Web site[80]. Understand fully the health situ-

---

80   http://www.DavidSolie.com

ations of your parents. Be a partner with them as it relates to their medical situations. They took care of you and knew everything about you when you were growing up; now is your chance to do the same for them.

How You Can Help

Your help doesn't end with just organizing what's already going on. Understanding illnesses, diagnoses, medications, and the entire maze of the current healthcare system is difficult enough for the best of us. Now add on top of that the fact that your parents might be confused and/or scared.

In short, what your parents need is an advocate. Someone who will help them navigate the world of health and healthcare. This person can be either you or another sibling or a family friend or even a professional who's been hired for just this purpose. The point is, there needs to be a quarterback on the team. Early on, this may be one of your parents. But as they age and their conditions get more complex, they may need help.

Consider the following areas for the quarterback's influence:

- Help organize the above medication and medical professional lists.
- Make sure other family members are aware of any issues and where they can get more information if you're not around.
- Help your parents prepare for their next medical appointments. For example, write out any questions you all have. If you write them out, you won't forget. As uncomfortable as all this may be, sometimes things don't go as they should in medical centers and hospitals. The quarterback needs to make sure that the issues for treatment are addressed and taken care of.
- Follow up on insurance, Medicare, Medicaid paperwork, reimbursements, etc.

Understanding that each medical professional involved is part of one greater team will help the quarterback organize and maintain a good healthcare experience. We can't just assume our primary physician will "take care of everything." Doctors are busy people. So while they may mean the best, don't expect them to be covering every angle. Understand that you or another family member will have to be the quarterback. Have your parents understand this and agree to this "team structure" earlier rather later, for their good and your own.

Dr. Monica Williams-Murphy is an emergency room physician and author of the book *It's Okay to Die*. She claims part of the problem we see in healthcare today is due to the fact doctors themselves fall victim to the habit of using the same pills and procedures no matter what the bigger, holistic picture of the patient.

Specifically, Dr. Williams-Murphy is concerned with end-of-life care and the needless and potentially harmful rote procedures physicians put their patients through. In a recent article she describes a hospice patient on 20 different medications. Although this woman had less than six months to live, she was being prescribed drugs like high cholesterol pills that had no chance of helping her long-term (she was going to die) but had the potential to do unnecessary harm. They also increased the overall cost of her care. Dr. Williams-Murphy said nearly half of the medications this poor woman was on could have been deleted from her regimen.[81]

In Dr. Williams-Murphy's words, "We have got to start practicing conscious, rational and caring medicine at the end of life. We doctors must ask ourselves, 'What medications really matter for this patient?' We must be having conversations that the patients and families can actually understand. We must be talking about how the 'high tech' pathway at the end of life may actually create or prolong unnecessary suffering. We must instead focus on communicating that the 'high touch,' comfort-focused pathway is most likely to give final peace to all parties—patients and families alike."

You can help by keeping your parents' medication details up-to-date and by getting them to ask questions of their healthcare providers. What's every medication for and is it absolutely necessary given the current circumstances? That question alone is a great starting point.

---

81 Dr. Monica Williams-Murphy, "Doctors are practicing irrational medicine at end of life," September 22, 2012, http://www.kevinmd.com/blog/

18

For Caregivers

Looking after the people we love as they grow old is part of life's journey. It's our time to show loyalty, love, kindness, and our ability to give. However, it can also be a grueling experience, and can chip away at our own relationships, money, and health.

In short, caregiving isn't for sissies. Yet, the odds are that many of us will become a caretaker at some point in our lives. As our parents age, they need more and more help looking after themselves. It may be one spouse having to care for the other or both parents or the one parent who now alone. It's only logical that we'll fulfill at least some, if not all, of that role.

However, we can prepare our parents and ourselves for this journey and make sure it flows as smoothly as possible for all parties concerned. Caregiving doesn't need to be a burden. It can be what it's meant to be, the sign of your love for your family.

Let's look at the role of the caregiver and how you can make it work in the best way possible.

Walk a Mile in Their Shoes

First off, if caregiving isn't for sissies, then getting old certainly isn't either. Most of us have experienced some of the symptoms: a new set of wrinkles, aches when we stand or first get moving in the morning, not bouncing back as quickly from a cold or late night out. The list goes on. Now ramp that up by ten and you'll begin to get the idea of what your parents might be feeling.

As we age, illnesses and disease can set in, even if not chronic. We find we're taking more medicines. Maybe our knees and hips are more irritable. This is the process of losing control physically, and it isn't a bit of fun. When your parents get to the stage where they actually need help with day-to-day living, they've lost a lot of control.

Remember, then, that your parents are struggling with the aging process, too. Most likely they're not happy with the idea of needing to be "looked after." Would you?

So, the first step on the caregiver journey is to sit back and imagine what it must be like to be in your parents' shoes. This will help you understand what they need and also become more deeply aware of what they're going through psychologically. Empathy goes a long way in showing love.

Getting Started on the Right Foot

Most of us haven't been trained to be professional caregivers. We didn't take classes on it, don't have a certification, and most probably aren't getting paid for it. So how do we actually do this caretaking thing?

Consider the following first steps:

- Research the disease(s) and/or illness(es) that your parents are experiencing. Knowledge is empowering, and the more you understand what's going on, the better able you'll be able to deal with it.

- Join caregiver communities. You can do this online or within your community. Many caretaker organizations exist with the sole purpose of helping other caretakers.

- Remember to look after yourself. You can't do it all. You'll need help, and the sooner you start getting other people on board, the better.

- You may feel anger or resentment at having to change your life to help your parents. Don't deny these feelings and shove them away somewhere dark to resurface their ugly heads later. Rather, find someone to talk to about your feelings. You're not alone. Your caregiver community will be a great source of support here.

Build Your Team

At the beginning of your caregiving journey, life may be easy. Your parents may be able to do most everything, and you just need to fill in a couple of gaps. However, chances are that as they age, you will need to spend an increasing amount of time helping them out. Plan on this. Build your team from the beginning.

First, assess who else is willing and able to help. If you're the only family member, then you will need to consider getting help from friends and/or caregiving professionals.

It may feel awkward asking for help, but on the other hand, you may be surprised at how many people are more than willing to chip in. Many times people want to help but don't know how.

Consider making a list of all the areas that your parents need help in. Then see whom on your team will be willing and able to help out in each area. Don't be afraid to ask friends and even church members. Many resources exist for you to get help from people who would be only too glad to help.

Create schedules, as in, Aunt Judy can take them bowling twice a month on Thursdays, or the neighbor will help do the grocery shopping once a week. Figure out what needs to be done, and then identify people to help fill the slots.

If you do need to eventually get professional caregiving help in the form of a nursing home or in-home assistance, you can minimize the amount needed if you already have a strong team.

Make sure everyone's role is clear, and understand that eventually each person will need a break, not the least of which is you.

Care for Yourself, Too

Caretaking is hard work and often goes unthanked and seemingly unappreciated. Given this, one of the most important people to look after is you. You can easily work yourself into a frazzle without even realizing it.

Watch for the following symptoms:

- irritability, even over minor issues or with the person you're caring for
- anxiousness
- depression
- constantly feeling tired
- catching every cold in town and not bouncing back quickly
- eating, smoking, or drinking more
- life has started to revolve around your caregiving role
- not exercising as much as you used to

Any and all of these can be symptoms of burnout. You must plan time off for yourself into your caretaking schedule. If you're not in good shape, it'll be that much more difficult for you to look after someone else. Chances are you have your own life and loved ones. Neglecting them won't help the situation at all. Don't let it negatively impact your own situation at home with your spouse and children. Planning early can help, but also recognizing that there are resources and people who will help is something to remember. It may seem like you're in it alone, but by taking a step back, you can often find solutions in places that you hadn't considered.

The most important step you can take toward looking after yourself is getting help in the caretaker role. If this is impossible, you still need to carve out the time to look after yourself, even if it's only 30 minutes a day.

Consider the following:

- Don't neglect your social life and connections. Friends are worth their weight in gold when times are tough.
- Exercise. This is one of the best ways to relieve stress and up your energy.
- Eat right and avoid the temptation to skip meals or stop at the fast food drive-in on the way home.

- Get enough sleep. Sleep deprivation has its own set of problems, and you don't need to be adding these into your life.
- Don't turn to alcohol, drugs, or overeating.
- Get involved in caregiver communities. With this support alone, you will feel like an enormous weight has been lifted from your shoulders.
- Your church community or even local senior center can be a resource for assistance. Don't be afraid to seek it out for help. You will actually be helping someone who wants to help.

Abusive Elderly Parents

We've all heard about it, and some of us have experienced it firsthand: older people taking out their frustrations and anger on the people they love and/or are helping them the most, specifically those who are their caregivers.

Sometimes this is the result of dementia or other cognitive decline. Other times the person simply feels comfortable behaving the way he feels when with his family. What he's really expressing is his frustration with the loss of control that comes with aging. A third cause could be that the person may just have had a latent abusive personality and it's coming out more as he ages.

Let's look at ways to deal with an abusive elderly parent.

- The first step is to take a moment and try to identify the cause of the aggression and acting out. If the person is simply frustrated with aging, a good dose of empathy will go a long way.
- In line with the above, don't take the abuse personally. Understand other factors involved. Your mother or father hasn't actually stopped loving you. Many adult children have experienced this, not just you.
- Take a stand, but don't bluff. Show them, don't just tell them, that you have boundaries and their abuse is not acceptable. How you do this will depend on the circumstances. Maybe it means you take a few days off from seeing them. Remind them what life is like when you're not there. Often this will help very quickly. Or bring in out-

side help, even temporarily. Show the person that if they continue to be abusive, you will relinquish your role as caretaker and bring in a professional full-time. Or it might mean convincing your sibling to come over for a few days or weeks in a row. But let the abusive person know you have boundaries and will stick to them.

Being a caretaker is an enormously valuable role in helping those you love. But it can also be hard and sometimes thankless. If you don't look after yourself, you can't really help other people. Life is meant to be enjoyed. If you're tired and resenting this intrusion in your life, you won't be anywhere close to enjoying yourself.

Do your part, but not to the extent that it harms you, either physically or emotionally. Build your team, plan ahead, and the odds are in your favor you'll make this a positive journey.

In Summary

The benefits of attaining and maintaining physical health spread throughout your life. Through proper eating and exercising, you and your parents will feel better, think better, and enjoy a longer and higher quality life. Most importantly, it isn't that hard to do. It's simply a matter of gradually replacing unhealthy habits with healthy ones. The key is to make it enjoyable so you're looking forward to more of the same.

You can play a crucial role in helping your parents enjoy this last stage of their lives. By setting the example, you will extend and enhance your own life. Now that's a good deal. Remember to start gradually with small, positive changes. Then as those habits set in, create additional ones.

Always keep in mind your parents' key motivational factors: to maintain control of their lives and to understand and leave a legacy. Good health will directly and positively impact those goals. Remind them of this often and enjoy the fruits of your labor.

Section Four

Mental Attitude and the Talk

19

Attitude is Everything

So far we've covered two crucial aspects to a successful retirement: financial plentitude and stability, and physical health and wellbeing. However, this is a four-legged retirement chair we're sitting on. Without the next two legs, the success and safety of your parents or loved one's retirement can tip right over into failure.

This section covers one of the most important elements: mental attitude. Staying fit isn't just a physical thing; it's mental, too. Our minds and bodies are so tightly linked that a poor attitude will affect us physically, just as a poor body will affect us mentally. The good news is, like our bodies, we can exercise our attitudes so they become more and more conducive to a positive and healthy life.

A study by the National Council on Aging (NCOA) found that retirees with overall negative mental attitudes die five to seven years sooner than their more positive thinking counterparts. Five to seven years! This means a bad attitude is as dangerous as heart disease or smoking.[82]

First of all, a healthy mental attitude simply means you're going to enjoy life more. Who doesn't want that? But it's not just a matter of seeing life as a glass half full. Happier people are also better equipped to withstand the inevitable hard times. Life isn't easy. If someone promised you it would be easy,

---

82 John Wolfskill, "How to Make a Smooth Transition into Retirement," February 17, 2007, http://www.Helium.com

then ask for your money back! A healthy attitude smoothes the road ahead and makes life more enjoyable for everyone involved.

Keith J. Karren, Ph.D., of the Department of Health Sciences at Brigham Young University says that "happy people have better health habits, lower blood pressure, and feistier immune systems then less happy people. When you combine all this with Aspinwall's findings that happy people seek out and absorb more health risk information, it adds up to an unambiguous picture of happiness as a prolonger of life and improver of health."[83]

Life Happens

I've spent a lot of time discussing the wonders and excitement related to retirement in this book thus far. I'll continue to focus throughout this book on achieving the dreams that your parents have for their later years. For now, however, I need to discuss one of the realities of retirement and getting older.

Simply put, as our parents get older and more into their retirement years, they will lose friends and family. The deaths of loved ones and those near and dear to retirees can be devastating. These losses will impact the best retirement plan and can make the dream of retirement a nightmare.

The journey to write my previous book began when both of my parents died within six months of each other. In the introduction to that book, I wrote, "*In 2009, my dad died after a battle with prostate cancer. Six months later, my mom and our family enjoyed a beautiful Sunday afternoon on the back deck of my house. The next day, I had to take my mom to the hospital where she died two days later due to a toxic condition and colon cancer (which she had left untreated and had told none of her family or friends about).*"

One of the major steps that I took to write that book was to understand if there was proof that there's actually a high likelihood of a surviving spouse passing away soon after the death of the spouse.

My research on the topic led me to write that book which examines the ways to prevent this from occurring but I still wanted to definitively know if the following hypothesis is true: "When one elderly spouse dies, the remaining spouse is more likely to die soon after this death."

---

83 *Ibid.*

Many people related to me how they had lost their own parents in similar manners, within months of each other. Although there are many anecdotal and qualitative studies that can lead one to conclusions, I soon found there is actual quantitative data that proves that the "widowhood effect" is real, particularly for men.

Anita Craemer wrote that *"among elderly couples, according to Harvard University sociologists, men are 22 percent more likely to die shortly after the death of a spouse, compared with 17 percent for women. And a National Institute on Aging study found that race plays a part in the widowhood effect, with white partners aged 67 or older more likely than elderly African Americans to succumb early in bereavement."*[84]

In the Encyclopedia of Death and Dying (yes, everything exists online), the definition of a widower includes this: *"Much of the research suggests that there is a greater prevalence of mortality and morbidity among the spousal bereaved compared to those who are currently married. Many of these same studies further report that the risk of becoming physically ill or dying soon after the loss of a spouse is greatest for widowers. The fact that men tend to be older when their spouses die could explain some of these findings. Although mortality is less common among younger widowers, the difference between their mortality rates and those of their married counterparts is greater than what is observed among older age groups, especially within the first six months of bereavement."*[85]

Although the studies seem to bear out the reality of the "widowhood effect," the fact is that it doesn't mean a death sentence for the elderly widowed. Rather, there are many studies and examples of how seniors have been able to address their situation. Rather than losing hope (and thus their reason to live), they are doing what their deceased spouse would want them to do—continue to live and live fully.

That's why I feel that a critical part of the talk with your parents should focus on the need to have a positive belief system and address one's mental attitude in retirement. The grief of losing a spouse in retirement will be

---

84 http://seattletimes.com/html/health/2014154333_widow08.html
85 http://www.deathreference.com/Vi-Z/Widowers.html#b

overwhelming to people, especially those who are unable to lean on others for support or who don't have a strong social structure in their retirement.

As you've been reading, you know that I believe that finding happiness in retirement requires planning financially, physically, mentally, emotionally, and spiritually. It also requires retirees to become and stay involved with others and participate in activities that allow them to continue to grow. These support structures are vital to helping retirees weather the storms of loss that come with retirement.

The importance of a support structure, whether with family or friends, is crucial to the recently widowed (we'll discuss this in the next section). It's also important that they are afforded the ability to work through their grief. For the survivors, it's important to recognize that you can have a role here, even if it's just by being able to listen to and comfort the grieving (even though you may be going through a grieving process as well).

An article by Deborah Carr of Rutgers University found that most older people are "surprisingly resilient after the death of a loved one."

> "One analysis based on the Changing Lives of Older Couples (CLOC), a multiwave study of bereavement among spouses age 65 and older, found that nearly half (46 percent) of older widows and widowers were "resilient," showing no or few depressive symptoms at both 6 and 18 months after their loss. Rather than showing signs of denial, emotional inhibition, or delayed grief, these relatively symptom-free older adults believed that death was a part of life, and they took great comfort in memories of their deceased spouses."[86]

Her article goes on to state that *"of the 900,000 Americans who lose a mate each year, nearly three-quarters are 65 or older. Patterns of spousal loss mirror mortality patterns overall. The death rate, or the number of people who die in a given year per 100,000 in the population, increases sharply beyond age 65. Losing a spouse is simply inevitable for most older married couples."*

Yet, the finding that seems most interesting to me from Carr's article is the following: *"Yet these patterns also suggest that older bereaved spouses have*

---

[86] http://www.rci.rutgers.edu/~carrds/good_grief.pdf

an important coping resource that is seldom available to younger widows and widowers: friends, peers, and siblings who also are adjusting to such a loss. Older adults often "rehearse" for losing a spouse by watching their peers go through the same experience; they can turn to one another for wisdom, practical support, and camaraderie."

This data makes sense when you think of certain circumstances. Perhaps the surviving spouse spent the last few years, or decades, as a primary caregiver. In this case, despite their love for their spouse, the final passing may come as something that they've prepared themselves for. Of course, it's hard watching someone you love slowly die while being the one looking after them, but this has allowed for some preparation for the inevitable (but can anyone truly be prepared for just such an event?).

Finally, some older people may just have a better perspective on life after all their years of learning. The death of their spouse is upsetting, no doubt, but they move on from the crisis as they've been doing for their entire lives.

According to Carr, "studies of older widows and widowers concur that only 15-20 percent experience clinical levels of depressive symptoms in the months immediately following the death, while 25-45 percent report mild symptoms, and anywhere from 30-50 percent report no depressive symptoms. Depressive symptoms typically are measured as the number of times in the past week that a person felt sad, blue, lonely, and lacking energy and motivation."[87]

There is also a state called the "broken heart syndrome." This is where the surviving spouse experiences real, physical symptoms caused by the loss of their loved one. Typically, they experience chest pains and think they're having a heart attack. These symptoms are caused by days-long surges in stress hormones, including adrenalin. ALthough the syndrome can be life threatening, the symptoms are usually short-lived.[88]

Depression and an unhealthy mental state can shorten our lives and make what living we do miserable. Carr's article shows there are different

---

87 *Ibid.*
88 "'Broken Heart' Syndrome: Real, Potentially Deadly but Recovery Quick," Johns Hopkins Medicine, Office of Corporate Communications, February 9, 2005, http://www.hopkinsmedicine.org/press_releases/2005/02_10_05.html

ways of grieving. Although there is no right way or wrong way, we can learn that there are ways to help those we love to deal with the grieving period.

It will be a lengthy process, and we need to understand that everyone grieves in their own way. You can never really prepare for the loss of a loved one, but I do believe that with a healthy mental outlook and strong social network, we can bounce back that much more quickly.

Taking the Old Out of Aging

I'll be going over the details of how we can attain and maintain a healthy mental attitude in the rest of this chapter. In Section Five I'll also cover how staying involved in life, socially and otherwise, dramatically improves our lives. But for now, I've condensed the ideas down into a "cheat sheet" of ten key points that can help to create that positive attitude that is so important in our later lives. Consider these when you have the talk with your parents. Also use it in your own lives when thinking about your own future.

1) Exercise regularly. I covered this thoroughly in the previous section, but the concept cannot be over emphasized. Get up off the couch and go for a walk if you want to live longer and feel better.
2) Eat a healthy, balanced diet. Ditto from above.
3) Spend quality time with those you love. This is one of the fastest avenues to happiness.
4) Keep learning. It's a great way to keep the mind fresh and alert.
5) Take up new hobbies and activities. Push your envelope and you'll see how interesting it can be.
6) Remember to laugh. Find the fun in life and it will begin to become part of who you are.
7) Keep up your friendships and social connections. This can take some effort, but it's effort well-spent, and is a great way to stay healthy mentally.
8) Follow your dreams. Why wait any longer? Seize the day and seize the opportunity.

9) Be open to new ideas and ways of seeing the world and experiencing life.
10) Plan your time. This will ensure you cover all the points above.

Having the Mental Attitude Talk

Now, obviously, you don't want to sit down and say, "Gee, mom and dad, I just want to make sure you don't go nuts on me." Broaching the subject of having a positive mental attitude can easily fall into the "too touchy feely for me" category. Although the value of mental health has received more scientific validity and respect over the years, it can still be an awkward subject to discuss. This is especially true for people born into generations where discussing mental health was actually taboo.

As with all aspects of the talk, choose the time and place with care. If your parents are already happy and generally have positive attitudes, then the talk shouldn't be that difficult. They already understand intuitively the joy life has to offer and are incorporating it into their lives. In fact, maybe there's something *you* can learn from *them* if your glass tends toward the half-empty side.

A more challenging talk happens with those parents or loved ones who are struggling with aging. Not everyone enjoys this side of life, and they may be unhappy, frustrated, and/or depressed. Remember, your job isn't actually to get them to change. In the end, you're not responsible for how they live their lives. Rather, what you can do is show them how they can create a more enjoyable and fulfilling life. Educate them on how they can flip the switch from grumpy old man to a "far-out happening" older person. Use anecdotes when possible. And most importantly of all, remind them what fun is. Set the example and include your friends and family. The choice is then theirs as to what path they take.

Sometimes the talk will come naturally after a crisis, like the death of a parent's friend or a family member. This type of setback can clear the way for deeper discussions about what your parents truly want from the rest of their lives. You have a wonderful opportunity here to help them in their grief and to take those important steps to avoiding depressing thoughts about their own mortality. Take them to the movies, bake their favorite cookies, turn them on to a new iPad—whatever you can do to pique their interest in life. Remind them of all the good life has to offer, and that it's not gone despite the fact they've lost someone special.

Most importantly, having the talk about mental attitude can be done by presenting your parents with actions they can take, such as transitioning to retirement, leaving their legacy, organizing end-of-life plans, reassessing and solidifying spiritual beliefs, and actively pursuing passions. These all provide concrete steps to gain and maintain a healthy attitude.

20

Transitioning Into Retirement

Unsurprisingly, life as a busy worker bee is often totally different from that as a hammock swingin', martini sippin' retiree. Most of the time, people leap from one lifestyle to another without giving much thought to the jarring transition involved.

You will have met people who became so enamored with retirement that you wonder how they ever had time to work. They're no longer sitting behind their desk at the office where you could easily find them. Now they're golfing and traveling and volunteering, and they're now downright impossible to get hold of!

Other people seem lost upon entering this phase of life. Their interests and energy fade away, and they become a shell of who they once were. Often, people's ego and identity were tied to their work. Now that they no longer have an "important" role to play, they struggle to find who they are within the home.

Preparing for the change between one lifestyle and the other can help smooth this transition. As I said earlier, some don't need any help. They fit into retirement so easily, it's as if they were born for it. But for most of us, this seismic shift in who we are and how we spend our days can be planned for and organized.

Let's look at the various factors.

Knowing When to Go

Perhaps your parents are perfectly happy working and living the life they've always had. Money isn't a concern so they could retire at any time financially, but there's no real reason to do so. Or is there? Maybe deep inside, life has grown stale. Board meetings are too long, and they're tired of the business travel involved.

Maybe motivation lies on the other end of the spectrum. They see their grandkids exactly twice a year: one week over the holidays and another in the summer. Dave Jr. has entered high school, and Suzie has grown so much that your parents barely recognize her in pictures. Before your parents know it, their grandkids will have flown the coop. They'll have missed it all!

It may be the talk that helps them see the other side of life they're missing out on. Simply by having the conversation about when they're considering retiring, you can stimulate underlying concerns. As they begin to see deep-seated but yet to be recognized desires, positive change is stimulated.

Isolde Davidson, advertising director for the Illinois State Bar Association, said it this way: "It was simple mortality. I asked myself, 'Is this the way I want to spend the years I have left?' I decided the answer was, 'No.'"[89]

Davidson actually planned her retirement four years in advance and is leaving no stone unturned. Freelance writing, part-time work, and possibly going back to school are all in the cards for her.

The decision as to when to retire is different for all of us. But through the talk, you can help your parents understand what's really important in their lives and how to get there.

The New "Old Age"

Del Webb, the largest active adult community homebuilder in the United States, released a 2010 Baby Boomer Survey full of fascinating insights into

---

[89] Robert J. Derocher, "What's Next? Senior Staff Members, and Bars, Plan for Retirement," American Bar Association, Volume 31 Number 3, January-February 2007, http://www.americanbar.org/publications/bar_leader/2006_07/3103/next.html.

the attitudes and activities of baby boomer retirees. According to this survey, aging boomers feel that aging is a state of mind. Simply put, "age is nothing—attitude is everything!"[90]

Some of their key findings include:

- Boomers believe "old age" begins at 80!
- Eighty percent of boomers feel younger than their age. The primary reasons they give for this are "happiness" and "a good sense of humor." Both of these fall firmly in the mental attitude category.
- The highest priority in life wasn't money or status or even health. Rather, young and old boomers alike said "family and spouse." So maybe all those extra days in the office aren't worth it after all?
- Forty percent of boomers said they'd taken up a new hobby in the last few years. Those that hadn't often said they were simply too busy doing other things to add one more to the list.
- On average, 72% of boomers will keep on working at some level during retirement. Financial concerns weren't the only factor. Many boomers simply want to stay busy and involved. Working part-time or in another occupation is one way of achieving this.[91]

What the Del Webb statistics show is that aging and retiring don't necessarily fit the stereotypical image we were raised with. Retirees today are active, busy, fit, and enjoying life more than ever before. This is the goal for both you and your parents. Having the talk early and planning ways to get the most out of retirement will work wonders for everyone.

How Ready Are You?

So how ready are your parents for retirement? They might have it all planned out or they might think they'll never retire and need you to help them see the light or they may fall anywhere in between.

---

90 *2010 Del Webb Baby Boomer Survey,* http://www.dwboomersurvey.com
91 *Ibid.*

Wherever your parents land in the spectrum above, you can help them transition into retirement smoothly and enjoyably. I've outlined six steps below to get retirement right the first time out of the gate.

Go through these steps with your parents as the talk progresses. Maybe they want to consider them privately. Some of the subjects will bring up deep feelings and dreams. And maybe they'll want you right there helping them figure out a vision of their future. It's fun watching someone create their lives. And remember, before long you'll be doing exactly the same thing.

Step One: Ask your parents to take some quiet time and think long and hard about what they want their retirement to be like. How do they want to spend their days and where? Ask them to picture their lives not just when they retire, but also one, five, ten, and twenty years down the road.

What specific goals do they have for retirement? Volunteering? Going back to school? Learning to scuba dive? It all counts.

Then, and this is critical, have them write it down. The very act of writing helps solidify the thoughts in their heads, and it also gives them—and you—something to go back to year after year.

Step Two: Add a dose of realism to the above picture. Sorry, but bad things happen in life, and we handle them best with planning. Deaths, divorces, financial calamities—which are most likely in your parents' world?

It can be difficult asking your parents to think about what their lives would be like without each other, but this is an important aspect of the talk. Consider bringing it up through an anecdote or humor. Tell them stories you know, such as the one about Harry taking up skydiving after he had lost his wife and, in no time at all, how he was loving life again.

It's okay to ask your parents what they would envision their life being if something happened to their spouse. More than likely, they've already had the conversation in private between the two of them. Discussing it with you at this point will allow you to "nudge" your parents later when you find the need to say things like, "Remember, Mom, that Dad said he wanted you to enjoy life if something happened to him."

Step Three: Write down a routine. One of the most common hiccups I hear about transitioning to retirement is it takes time to get used to all that… time. Your parents won't have to structure themselves like they were back at work, but scheduling in exercise, hobbies, dinners cooked together, and more will help provide a sense of order that work normally provides.

I know that this was very important to my parents. My mother, who worked nights for many years, enjoyed her sleep, but my father was used to waking up early. So each morning my dad would get up before her, walk the dog, and go to the store to get the local papers, which he would read before my mom woke up.

Developing a routine like this or meeting a friend for lunch each week or implementing a walking program with a friend helps the transition to retirement. You can assist your parents by creating a list of routines that will work for them.

Step Four: Write down proactive steps for achieving the life they envisioned in Step One. If their goal is to RV their way across America, when will they buy the RV? Where will they park it when they're not traveling? How long will they spend on this adventure? What will they do with the cat?

The deeper they dig into this life they've pictured, the more real it will become. By writing down actual steps toward achieving it, they're leaps closer to making it reality. Besides, it's fun watching dreams hatch.

This may necessitate some realistic discussions about their financial situation and plans. You can play a role that either warns or encourages your parents to pursue these goals. If buying an RV will make a negative impact on their finances going forward, you can raise the need for them to consider their current and future expenses before pursuing this purchase. Likewise, our parents may not realize that they can actually afford some luxuries, and you may need to play a role to "push" them into taking the dive into their dreams by opening their wallets when their finances can well support such purchases.

Step Five: As you know I've broken down retiring successfully into the Four Keys to a safe retirement: financial preparedness, physical health, mental attitude, and staying involved. Ask your parents to discuss the keys, and then write down how they will address each of these in their retirement.

One of the best things you can do is to ask them to develop plans for themselves in each of these areas. Along with their financial plan, ask them how they will develop and implement a plan for their health, their attitude, their need to stay involved, and even their spiritually journey over the next few years. It doesn't need to be a joint plan; it can be two separate plans for each parent.

For example, maybe your mom will take up yoga and your dad will start walking when golfing. Or they'll both enroll in a class in the local community center. Or they'll form a bridge club in which they and their friends will share the hosting. These plans don't have to be fixed in stone, but it gets everyone thinking about how to go about getting the most out of retirement.

Step Six: Looking after yourself mentally is no less important than looking after yourself financially. Therefore, when your parents do their own annual financial review, have them book time to do a review of these steps as well. Have them call it their "Dream Retirement Plan," or whatever works for them. Just have them agree to revisit these plans annually.

Then sit back and watch your parents truly enjoy their Golden Years.

21

Leaving a Legacy

As I've mentioned previously in this book, as we age, two priorities stand above all others: the need to maintain control of our lives and the need to understand the legacy that we'll leave behind.

As David Solie puts it, "Every day, whether they are millionaire moguls or retired postal clerks, former CEOs or homemakers par excellence, our elders are engaged in an elaborate process of reviewing their lives to find something of meaning that will last long after they depart."

He continues, "Once they feel that control is no longer an issue, senior adults focus on reviewing their lives to find what it meant for them to have lived."[92]

Your job, then, is to help your parents to deeply understand their legacy. What were their lives all about? At the end of the day, what was most important to them?

One excellent way of helping is to simply ask them questions about their life and let them work out the levels of importance. This is what the process is all about at its origin. And helping them will be good for you, too. We tend to think of our parents as only filling that role of parenting, but actually, they've worn just as many hats as you have—maybe more. Encourage them to talk about their lives, what they achieved, and how they did it.

In the course of writing this book, I was amazed at the wealth of resources that are available to people and families interested in compiling leg-

---
92 Solie, How to Say It to Seniors, Op. cit., p. 36

acies.[93] One of the leaders in the area of helping others to create legacies is the Legacy Project.[94] It has a resource called "Across Generations," which has the following mission:

> "Across Generations explores our connections with others and, in particular, encourages closer relationships between generations. How can we grow up and grow old with meaning and dignity? How can we celebrate the unique, special relationships that can be forged between young and old, and bring the generations closer in our families and communities? How can these relationships make a real difference in individual lives and in communities?"[95]

As part of this resource, they include questionnaires that can be used when interviewing our older family members. Here are some questions that can be great conversation starters when having a "legacy conversation"[96] with your own parents:

- Can you describe the neighborhood you grew up in?
- What was best gift you received growing up?
- What did you want to be when you were growing up?
- Who was your best friend when you were growing up?
- Who has been the most significant person in your life?
- What was the happiest time in your life?
- What has been your greatest accomplishment?
- If you could change anything at anytime in your life, what would it be?
- What are you most thankful for?
- Share with us a story that you've never told us.

I've also heard from adult children who have gone through this process, that another way to dig deeper is to encourage their parents to ask questions

---

[93] http://safe4retirement.com/working-with-your-parents-to-create-a-legacy
[94] http://www.legacyproject.org/index.html
[95] http://www.legacyproject.org/programs/acrossgen.html
[96] http://www.legacyproject.org/guides/lifeintquestions.pdf

of each other. Among some of the questions that I've heard couples asking of each other are the following:

- What would you do in retirement if you were not worried what anyone else might think about it?
- Is there anyone whose retirement you admire? Do you hope yours will be like theirs? What about their retirement do you wish to emulate?
- What's your "bucket list"?

These are not only questions that will help your parents to understand more about what they want in their retirement, but it'll allow them to know each other even better.

Imagine that! Providing an opportunity for your parents to learn new things about each other after all of these years can be a priceless experience.

A Legacy of People

Leaving a legacy isn't just a celebration of the commercial or work successes we've created, although for many of us these have enormous value. Our legacy is also in large part a reflection of the people we love and have loved in our lives. Humans are social creatures. We're wired to experience deep relationships throughout our lives. Some of the most poignant have been with our family, but we've also forge deep relationships with friends.

This socialness also leads us to influence and be influenced by such people as colleagues, acquaintances, and even complete strangers.

I had a random conversation with an elderly woman at the gym that I'll never forget. Although I never saw her again, her words resonate with me still today. I heard later that she was the widow of a multimillionaire and had recently suffered the loss of both her husband and their youngest child.

"We're all climbing the same mountain," she calmly said. In other words, all the money in the world wouldn't bring back the people she loved the most.

Love—the giving and receiving of it—is one of the most fundamental and, therefore, most important parts of life. Who in this world doesn't want to be loved, to feel special, to be separated from the other seven billion people in the world as unique and worth loving? Everyone wants this.

Part of your parent's legacy, therefore, is helping them delve into their past and remember the people who made a difference.

I spoke to a retired executive recently about what he valued most from his work. He'd risen from truck-driving delivery boy to one of the top leaders in an international firm. His path had included heading branches and districts, making corporate acquisitions, and eventually running this firm's enterprises in entire countries. In the process, he raised three beautiful daughters and accumulated plenty of money.

I asked him what he loved most about his work. Was it watching the bucks roll in? Nope.

Hobnobbing with the CEO and other top executives? Not a chance.

Sending his children to the finest schools? Not bad, but not at the top of the list.

Instead, what was most important about his work was "helping people grow. The specific business didn't matter, what turned me on was helping someone achieve success—building their career, buying their home, sending their kids to college."

This is a great example of the human aspect of leaving a legacy. Sure he's proud of having climbed so high and achieving so much, but what he remembers and values the most are the individuals he helped along the way.

Talk to your parents about the people who have stood out in their lives. Who did they give a hand to? Who helped them along the way? What words of wisdom did they overhear that subtly influenced their life forever? This is all part of their legacy and is of immense importance to them at this stage of their lives.

You can help by doing one of the rarest things of all: listening.

Writing It Down

A writer friend of mine told me a story about an autobiography she was ghost-writing for a client. This rising businessman—let's call him Mark—wanted to tell his story: from scraping out a living with his family as a kid to graduating from college to achieving his financial and personal goals and dreams. Mark hoped his story would inspire new entrepreneurs to fulfill their dreams, too. Little did he know what treasures lay within his own family.

As my friend asked Mark questions about the important people in his life, he talked often about his grandmother, who had left a deep and inspiring impression on him. With no hesitation he knew he could never have achieved what he did without her wisdom influencing him as a child. Unfortunately, while working on the book, Mark's grandmother died. As funeral preparations were being made, Mark received a call notifying him that his grandmother—that humble, giving, always-putting-other-people-first person—was eligible for a 21 gun salute burial in Arlington Cemetery.

Mark was stunned. However, with a little digging he found out his grandmother had been on-duty as a nurse at Pearl Harbor on December 7th, 1941, the day the Japanese air force attacked. She'd worked relentlessly serving the wounded and dying soldiers on that terrible day. The crazy thing is, she never told anyone. Sure, he sort of remembered she'd been a nurse in the war, but no one knew the specifics or what personal risks she'd taken to save the lives of soldiers on one of the most infamous days in American history.

Your parents, too, have their own "gems" of stories. Encourage them to write down these stories. This is a healthy and long-lasting way to leave a legacy. Not only do your parents get to fully nurture their stories and fill out the details, but also the entire family is left with a written legacy.

I promise you'll hear amazing stories that will open new windows into whom your parents really are. I think of the time when I asked my dad in his later years about his experience in the Navy. He was on an aircraft carrier called the USS *Guadalcanal*. His job was to work on the deck where the planes landed.

One night, while on the deck, he was standing with another Navy man when the cable that caught the planes when landing snapped. The man standing next to him was significantly injured when the cable hit him. I was amazed by a story that was obviously traumatizing to him but was news to me. So I asked my dad what he did after this. He told me, "After it happened, I walked down to the kitchen and requested a job there, and I ended up cooking on the ship for the rest of my tour of duty."

By asking your parents these types of questions, you'll gain new insights into who they are, and believe me, they'll love talking about it.

Another way to write it down, sort of, is to encourage your parents to make scrapbooks or even recordings. For more visual or audio people, this can be a more direct route to telling their stories. Help them organize scrapbooks and putting together the pictures and bits and pieces of lives gone past. Or show them how to create a YouTube video recording of them telling the story of catching the rogue bull that wandered into their backyard that Christmas day.[97]

You may be saying to yourself, "How will I have time for this too? I barely have enough time to run my own life." Executor's Resource points out that "interviewing and recording your parents or relative sounds easier than it is. Many parents will tell you their story isn't important despite assurances that it is. Additionally, without a third party to do the interview, family baggage and judgment can get in the way."[98]

There are actually many outside resources that can help in recording legacies for your family. This will save you time and might encourage your parents to speak more openly. Lettice Stuart was an accomplished writer and reporter with *The New York Times* who had all the skills necessary to record the legacies of her family: "their stories, their thoughts and feelings about death, life and family."[99] Unfortunately, she lost both of her parents in the course of two years and never had the opportunity to hear their stories. So in 1996 she started her business, Portraits in Words, to help people record what

---

97 See George Carlin's "Legacy Interview" on YouTube at http://www.youtube.com/watch?v=J05K-Fn7OSo
98 http://www.executorsresource.com/docs/howtoconductalegacyinterview.pdf
99 *Ibid.*

she did not. Portraits in Words produces both printed books and videos that capture family memories.[100]

You can also find someone at the Web site for the Association of Personal Historians.[101] (Now doesn't that sound like a group of people who are not only good listeners but have heard many great stories? Not a bad way to earn a living, I think!) Their vision is of "a world in which the story of every person, family, community, and organization is recorded and preserved." Not a bad vision to aspire to.

However you choose to capture the legacy of your parents, remember that it's fundamental to easing them into a successful retirement and it'll provide joy for both you and them. I assure you that you'll not only learn something about them, but about yourself as well.

Living Inheritances

Leaving a financial legacy is often part of big-picture retirement planning, as I discussed in Section Two. It's virtually impossible, and way too risky, to spend your last penny the day you die. However, many retirees want to see their beneficiaries enjoying the fruits of their labors. It seems silly to them to work hard to accumulate their money but never get to witness the help it will bring to those they love.

Therefore, leaving a financial legacy while still living is something many retirees look into. Not only does it provide tax benefits, but its stipulations can be tacked onto receipt of the funds.

For example, one of my clients formed trusts for his children with different levels of assets received dependent upon benchmarks achieved, such as college graduation, graduate school, career-oriented employment for X number of years, etc. The idea wasn't to force his children into a rigid structure, but rather to make sure they were heading in a responsible direction and, therefore, not abuse the money.

The greatest advantage for many, however, is being able to watch their loved ones benefit from their legacy, such as buying their first house, getting

---

100 http://www.portraitsinwords.com
101 http://www.personalhistorians.org/index.php

them started in their own business, or taking them on the cruise of a lifetime. All are valid and meaningful ways to explore leaving a financial legacy.

How exactly to bring this up with your parents without sounding tacky is the tricky bit? Perhaps what's best is to simply know it's an option to finding out what your parents want to do. You and or your financial advisor can throw out other options, and your parents will respond to what feels right to them.

Legacies Yet to be Realized

Although I'm encouraging you to talk to your parents and help them reexamine their lives, I also want you to encourage them to keep creating new memories and adding on to their legacies. A great way to do this is to facilitate strong relationships with their grandchildren.

Grandparents and grandchildren have special relationships to begin with. It comes with the territory. Grandparents can spoil the kids more easily, and they provide an endless source of stories and knowledge that might not be received as well from parents. My mom used to have a sign up in her home that said, "Many children are spoiled because you can't spank Grandma."

Children, on the other hand, are excellent at keeping those around them young and on their toes. How many crazy, yet timelessly wise, things have your own children or grandchildren said and done?

I bring this subject up because it's near and dear to my heart. I was lucky enough to have great experiences with my grandparents when I was young. Although my dad's parents had passed on before I was born, I was lucky to have my mom's wonderful parents spend so much of their time with my sister and me. They weren't a rich couple, and although my grandfather ran a business (and planted the entrepreneurial gene in me), they never owned a home.

I remember the bizarre times I had as a child with them when they lived above a New York City tavern. Holiday meals would be interrupted by some "friend" coming up the stairs looking for something to eat or seeking another drink, and no one was ever turned away. One of the rewards for my grandparents' generosity was when a horn-based band came up the stairs to play us a few songs while my grandfather shared his New Year's scotch with all of them.

These were great times that are now part of the legacy they left me with. I relish those memories and think of my own kids, who are in their early teens and have already lost all of their grandparents. Although they're gone, we still have many joyful talks about their grandparents and all the silly and wonderful things they shared with us.

Perhaps you find that geography and hectic lives don't always make it easy to keep your children involved with your parents. But if and when you can, expanding your parent's legacies to include your own children is excellent for everyone involved. You get a break, your kids get loved and entertained, and your parents tap into deep levels of happiness and connection. That's a win-win-win for everybody that can last a lifetime!

22

Gaining Peace of Mind

End-of-life talks will be some of the most difficult and awkward discussions we'll ever have. They're right up there with being told about the birds and bees, or the time you broke the news to Mom and Dad that you and their new car were in just a bit more than a little fender-bender.

However, the cruel fact is, we're all going to eventually die. We can extend life through good health, habits, and attitudes, but the end for each of us remains the same. We don't like to think about it, but eventually our parents will die.

Because of this stubborn fact, it's extra-important to fully explore end-of-life subjects in the talk, not only where your parents want to live in retirement or how they want to live, but also you need to ask them how do they want to address a living will or where do they want to be buried. These are important and necessary questions, and I fully understand that they aren't easy ones to bring up.

As I stated in Section One, approximately 70% of people currently over the age of 65 will need long-term care of some type at some point. Add to this that more than 40% will end up in a nursing home, many of who will need more than five years of long-term care.[102]

These facts make a strong case for having the talk about end-of-life issues. You need to understand what your parents want. This way you can

---

102 Sue Shellenbarger, "'The Talk' With Mom and Dad," *The Wall Street Journal*, February 23, 2011

make sure, to the best of your ability, that their wishes are carried out if they're not able to manage things for themselves.

On the other hand, they gain peace of mind knowing that you understand both how they want to live their lives and how they want to finish those lives. By this I mean, who has the durable power of attorney to handle medical and financial decisions should they become incapacitated? How much ongoing medical assistance do they want should the pull-the-plug subject become necessary? Is the living will completed? Finally, what do they want done with their remains?

Let's go through the process of the end-of-life talk step by step.

How to Have the Talk

As with all aspects of the talk, first and foremost, put yourself in your parent's shoes. In this case consider the following:

- What are their deepest fears about aging? About becoming ill and/or incapacitated? About pain? About moving from the family home to a care facility? About death?
- What will be most important to them in their final years?
- What considerations have they made regarding a living will?
- What sort of help do they want and expect from their family?[103]

By truly imagining what life must look like from their vantage point, you will be much more receptive to their wishes and concerns. The point is to understand what they want and to help facilitate it in the best way possible.

If you're nervous about initiating the end-of-life talk, consider turning the table and discussing your own decisions first. Go out and get your own will made (if you don't have one already, you should) and tell them about it. Tell them that if you should ever become medically incapacitated, you've designated so-and-so to make your decisions for you. Let them know you understand these are huge decisions and responsibilities and you want them involved. Doing this is a natural and easy segue into asking them what they've done in their own situation.

---

[103] Eric N. Holk, "The Talk You Must Have With Your Parents," http://www.trusts-etc.com/talkyoumusthave.html, 2012

Remember to emphasize that making these choices early is actually very empowering. You're in control of these critical decisions, rather than leaving them to chance.

You can also instigate and steer this conversation by bringing in a third party in the form of a financial advisor or estate planning attorney. Sometimes having a nonfamily member bring up awkward subjects takes the pressure off both parties. Besides, these are professionals who should be familiar with what to ask and how to make sure all areas are covered.

Another point to remember is that sometimes Dad will assume the role of decision maker, leaving Mom on the sidelines. If she's been a homemaker all her life, this may seem a perfectly logical process. However, remember that women more often survive their husbands rather than the other way around. Chances are she'll be the one left to make decisions after he's gone. Therefore, make sure your mom is involved and her wishes are heard just as loudly as anyone else's.

And sometimes your parents will have it all taken care of already. Their wills will be drawn and up to date, their trusts will be in order, and they'll have medical and financial directives all worked out. In this case, you just need to be filled in on the facts should a time arrive when they're incapacitated and can't tell you themselves. Just because they've "got it all handled" doesn't mean you shouldn't know what their decisions are. Explain to them that you don't want to change anything or take control, you just want to know what's going on beforehand.

Consider these issues before you begin the talk:

- Do your research beforehand. This might mean being able to refer a quality estate planning attorney, provide information on assisted-living communities, and/or speak knowledgably about medical directives.
- Unless you've been designated the quarterback in this realm, make sure other family members know what you're discussing and what the decisions are.
- Consider the timing and location. Make sure it's comfortable and private, like in their home.

- Listen. Listen. Listen. This isn't about you. It's about your parents.
- Agree to revisit the subjects during their annual financial and retirement review.

What to Include in the Talk

Many of various talk subjects overlap. This is just fine because all the decisions need to dovetail. I've listed below eight points to cover in the end-of-life talk. This is a starting point. Tailor the talk to your specific circumstances, but be sure to cover at least these subjects. If you've done so in earlier talks (and you will have), just bring up how they're important here, too.

1. Do they have a will and any other estate planning? If so, when was it last updated?
2. Do they have an advance health care directive and living will along with a durable power of attorney for financial matters? Who is responsible for making financial and health care decisions should either or both of them become incapacitated?
3. Where do they keep the above documents and any other financial documents that will have been covered in the financial talk?
4. When and where would they consider moving?
5. What type of memorial service would they like?
6. Are they organ donors?
7. How much help do they want and expect from you and other siblings, family members, and/or friends?
8. What other concerns, fears, and wishes do they have in light of this conversation?

If either of your parents is suffering from dementia, this talk can be more difficult. They may become confused or scared or incorrectly believe you're after something. But it's also all the more important that these issues are taken care of while your parents are still able to make sound decisions. Sooner is better. You must make sure that all the legal documents are written up while they're still capable of expressing their wishes.

Given all these rather scary factors, it's clear why having the talk is so critical. Honoring the last phases of life, as unattractive and difficult as they may be, show the deep respect and love you have for your parents.

What will happen as you go though these items is your parents will actually achieve peace of mind when they recognize that someone who loves them will follow their wishes. Don't discount this. In fact, think of this when you're stumbling over whether to bring the subject up for the first or fifth time. Doing it may bring discomfort to you and your parents, but when it's done, there's a calm, settledness that you and your parents will achieve.

After my dad had his first experience with cancer, my parents actually did the right things by sitting down with estate attorneys to prepare their wills and deal with financial matters. Fortunately, this was done well before he passed on, not within the "look back" period of a trust, so their ability to move assets under our names became a moot point.

Rightfully so, they were very proud when they informed my sister and me that they had done that. We thanked them as they told us the details of their plans. They commented how they felt they now had peace of mind about this topic because they had done it and discussed it with us.

However, all the end-of-life details of their plans were not as clear cut. We talked somewhat about funeral arrangements, and although they had done well to do a living will, we knew little about questions such as long-term care, nursing home considerations, and charitable wishes. Most of these things we never knew when they died, and we made decisions based on what we thought was best.

As it was for my parents, it's a lot to ask for most parents to consider all of these things at one time. That's why it's important to remember that this is all a process. Doing a will is great. Writing up a living will is terrific. Deciding what will happen at the time of death is, for many parents, a situation that should probably not be bundled together with these other items.

Allow your parents the time to do all these things. The key here is to get the process started and remember that this is a difficult part of the talk, probably the toughest. But it doesn't have to be done all at once. What's important is to have your parents view you as a resource and influencer who will pursue these questions when they feel most comfortable. By arming yourself with the right questions and topics, as I've provided here, you'll have what you need to help them. You'll supply the most important aspect needed for this discussion: love.

The Joys of Friends

On a lighter note (whew!), let's discuss some of the more entertaining ways your parents can create a successful retirement.

David Counts, Ph.D., a professor of anthropology at McMaster University, states there are three areas critical to a successful retirement: have control of your life, have interesting and challenging things to do, and have friends outside the family.[104]

I've discussed the importance of your parents feeling in control of their lives and decisions. Along with leaving a legacy, this is a hot spot for the aging. As I've mentioned previously, having interesting and challenging things to do help stimulate a positive attitude and also help folks stay involved, which I'll discuss at length in the next section. But it's the value of having friends outside the family that I'd like to emphasize in this chapter.

Friends don't just make life more fun, although that's a huge benefit; they also extend life itself. Thomas Foster, Ph.D., of Kent State University is a professor in the Department of Adult, Counseling, Health and Vocational Education. He studied how a person's attitude toward retirement affects their overall wellness.

Foster found that the two largest predictors of wellness in retirement were depression and attitude toward retirement. Approximately 38% of the variance in wellness scores was attributable to these two factors. In other

---

[104] John Wolfskill, "How to Make a Smooth Transition into Retirement," February 17, 2007, http://www.helium.com

words, if you're happy and have a positive attitude, you'll most likely be healthier, too.[105]

Interestingly, Foster found that income accounted for just 1% of the variance in wellness. Attitude was more important. There's a big lesson right there.

Family and Friends

Obviously, the first place your parents can go to nurture relationships is with family and current friends. However, this isn't always easy as people, especially those still working, are busy and leading their own lives. It's a common complaint that having less time for those we love is a by-product of our hectic lives.

Retired people, on the other hand, have more choice over their time. Your parents can use this to their advantage when it comes to strengthening family relationships. Consider discussing the following with them:

- Spend more time with their grandchildren. If this works out geographically, grandparents are great resources for child-sitting, weekend outing organizing, and sleepovers.

- If everyone in the family is busy, suggest to your parents that they take the leadership role in family get togethers. Maybe it's just a matter of bringing over a big pot of chili so your daughter doesn't have to cook that evening. Or maybe they could instigate weekly game nights, or monthly family excursions to somewhere new.

- Get them using social media. They may not be able to see their grandchildren who live across the country often enough, but they can friend them on Facebook, then like, comment, and post replies to what they're up to. They might even be labeled "cool" if they do this.

- Ask them about extended family members and encourage them to rekindle relationships.

---

[105] Thomas Wayne Foster, Ph.D., *Depression, Anxiety, and Attitude Toward Retirement as Predictors of Wellness for Workers Near Retirement*, Ohio Link ETD Center, 2008

- Get over past grudges and grievances. Life is short and leftover disputes or disagreements should be shoved to the side. No sensible person wants them and a simple greeting and invitation to lunch may be enough to mend old wounds.

Each of the above suggestions also applies to friends, old and new. The key is for your parents to understand the value of relationships in this phase of their life, and to actively pursue them. However, after decades in the workforce where new friends and acquaintances came with the job, it may take some practice to relearn how to make new friends.

Remember, those friendships from work may not stay as strong in the retirement world. Sometimes the common denominator is the profession, and when that's gone, you don't have as many things in common. This shouldn't be surprising, and it shouldn't be a problem as new friends are readily available to be made.

Ask your parents to consider the following:

- Join a club. Whether it's golf, tennis, bridge, or croquet, clubs provide a venue for people with something in common to gather and get to know each other. All this while pursuing an activity they enjoy. That's a good deal.

- Get involved in the community through volunteering. Encourage your parents to get out and become involved in where they live. It could be at their church, a nearby community center, or through Big Brothers Big Sisters. They may have been so busy with work and raising a family they never had the chance to check out the possibilities in their own backyard.

- Rekindle old friendships. As I mentioned above, sometimes your best friends are right there in front of you. You just haven't had the time to get to know them again.

- Use social networking. I'll go over this in greater detail in the next section. Once they get the hang of it, your parents will have fun with Facebook, Pinterest, iPads, and iPhones. Sites like Facebook are not only a great way to stay connected with family and especially with grandchildren, as I've earlier stated, but it's also a way to reconnect with old friends.

- Consider part-time work. I'll go over this and most of these topics more thoroughly in the next section, but in the context here, part-time work will get your parents connecting with new people, whether they need the money or not.

The success of your parents' retirement will increase dramatically when they have a robust network of friends. They'll be intellectually stimulated, actively participate in things they love, reminded of the value they have to offer others, and surrounded by new sources of love. Sounds like a pretty good deal to me.

Finding Romance After 50

Sad but true, many retirees will end up a widow or widower. It's just a fact of life that one-half of the team outlives the other. Add to this the increased rate of divorce for baby boomers, and we're looking at a lot of singles over the age of 50.

According to a study by Bowling Green State University, divorce rates for folks over 50 have more than doubled in the last 20 years. In 1990 less than 10% of over-50s were divorced, and in 2009 that rate had risen to 25%.[106]

When the children are gone and retirement looms near, people reassess what makes them happy. Susan L. Brown, coauthor of the Bowling Green study said, "We have high expectations for what constitutes a good marriage today and we're looking for self-fulfillment and individual happiness in our relationships. When you are 60-65 you retire and say, 'Well, I can live another 20, 25 years. Do I want to spend my life with that person? Is she or he making me happy?' And if not, well, divorce is a viable alternative."[107]

Can seniors find love again? Of course, it happens all the time. Many couples claim marriage or at least "shacking up" is better when they're older and know what they do and don't like.

---

106 Greg Clary and Athena Jones, "Baby Boomer Divorce Rate Doubles," June 24, 2012, http://www.CNN.com
107 *Ibid.*

The stigma of online dating is far less today than it once was. Perfectmatch.com, an online dating site, states that the over-50 segment is the fastest growing group of online dating subscribers. And those over 55 accounted for almost 17% of all traffic on online dating sites.[108] In many cases, their own grown children directed their parents to these online sites.

Match.com, the world's most popular online dating site, gives these tips for finding love in your 50s and 60s:[109]

- Get involved in community service, even if this means stepping outside your comfort zone.
- Put your opinion out there when at an audience-oriented event, even if you're not sure the other person will agree. You'll quickly learn the other person's point of view and how well he or she responds to debate and open mindedness.
- Visit new places. Go on a cruise or an organized tour or to an art or music festival. You're doing something you love and increasing the chances of meeting a like-minded person.
- Ask your friends if they know of anyone who's single and might be a fit for you. They might not have assumed you were thinking of and looking for romance.
- Check out reputable online dating sites. A recent study by match.com found that 17% of marriages in the last three years met online. It's now become the third most successful way to find a potential mate, behind only meeting through a mutual acquaintance or at work or school.[110]

It may seem strange trying to help your mother or father find another love interest. However, despite the fact they're your parent, they're just as human as the next person. We're happier when we're in a good relationship. It's the way we're wired. You can build enormous inroads on the way to a positive mental attitude by helping those you love find someone special.

---

108 "Dating Facts and Statistics," http://www.perfectmatch.com,
109 Elise Nersesian, "Finding love in your 50s and 60s," http://www.match.com,
110 Ellen McCarthy, "Marriage-minded do better online than at bars, survey claims," *The Washington Post*, April 25, 2010. Also available online at http://www.washingtonpost.com/wp-dyn/content/article/2010/04/23/AR2010042300014.html

24

The Importance of Beliefs

As we age, it's not at all unusual for our thoughts to veer toward the spiritual. We ponder what this life of ours has been all about.

· Harold G. Koenig, MD, author of *Purpose and Power in Retirement*, says, "Finding purpose is more urgent than ever during the retirement years, when the search for purpose becomes one of the deepest human longings."[111] Not only does a purpose give meaning to this journey, but it also energizes us for the last leg.

Finding a purpose in life and spiritual introspection are closely linked. For many people they're one and the same. When reflecting on the legacy of our lives, we ask ourselves questions like, "What was it all for? What's this thing called life about? What comes next after I die?"

Not surprisingly, these questions become more poignant the closer we come to our own mortality. In our 20s and 30s we feel invincible. Old age is too far away to even think about, and the fact we have friends and family turning the ancient age of 50 is beyond even considering. In our 40s we're too busy with kids and careers to really worry much about dying. But as we pass that number 50, and then even as our 60s and 70s roll around, we realize we have a distinctly limited number of years left.

It's at this point that it becomes vital to attach meaning to our lives. Understanding our legacy is part of this, as is coming to terms with our own spirituality. A *Newsweek* survey found that 56 percent of people between

---

[111] Harold G. Koenig, MD, *Purpose and Power in Retirement*, Templeton Foundation Press, 2002

40-59 described themselves as "both religious and spiritual,"[112] and that spirituality in their daily lives was very important. Yet for those over 60, this number increased to 66 percent. Not only are we a spiritual people, but this need also increases as we age.

Are You Spiritual or Religious?

Let's get this difference taken care of right away. The two concepts are similar, but have important differences, too. Being "religious" implies adherence to a spiritual doctrine, like an organized church or religion. Each religion has specific beliefs and practices associated with it that followers mostly abide by.

Spirituality, on the other hand, is a much wider concept that includes questions like, "Why are we here? Is there a higher power?" Whereas one usually goes to a specific location to practice their religion, spirituality can be accessed anywhere: in a quiet moment alone, a yoga class, meditating, on a walk close to nature, or any other peaceful place, even just taking a deep breath.

I think of it as religion being external and spirituality being internal. I'm more concerned with the spiritual, the internal, in this chapter. And I'm certainly not recommending or promoting any religion or practice. Those are personal choices each one of us must make as individuals. But I am strongly suggesting that a thorough assessment and understanding of spirituality is essential for a successful retirement.

The Mortality Factor

When I googled "spirituality," I was given 248 million search results to choose from. That'll keep the best of us busy for years! However, we all know what we mean by spirituality. We might think of it as that deep connection we feel with ourselves when we sit quietly and go inwards. Or it's the immense awe and respect we have for the beauty of nature. Neither of these acts and feelings is bound to one religion, but they take us closer to a deeper meaning—a spiritual one.

---

112 Jan Cullinane, "Retirement and Spirituality," National Association of Baby Boomer Women Web site, June 11, 2007, http://nabbw.com/associates/jan-cullinane/

As we age we collect more and more experiences brushing against mortality. We watch our body change, not usually for the better, and our minds slow and become forgetful. Our children will have left the nest and may be living far away, giving us the sense of a loss of family. And, importantly, we will have watched people around us die. By the time we reach our 50s and 60s we've most likely had a close relative or friend die—sometimes more than one.

All these experiences poke us right in the "what's it all about?" spot. Add to this the realization that we might be next, and a quest for spiritual peace and understanding is a natural.

Your parents are most probably going through this right now.

Your Role in Their Spirituality

Like so many aspects of helping your parents achieve a successful retirement, you can't—and shouldn't even try to—tell them how to live their lives or make decisions for them, unless it's absolutely necessary. If your parents ask for help and want you to take over control of some aspect of their life, that's one thing. But, otherwise, your role is that of a guide. And an important role it is.

You can serve as a guide in their search for spiritual meaning. Many people of older generations were raised with one set of spiritual beliefs and are hesitant, or feel guilty, exploring something new. By having the talk, you can become a catalyst for helping them to open up when it comes to matters of spirituality.

The importance of this is twofold. First, you need to understand their beliefs so that their end of life preparations and rituals are done according to their wishes. Second, and perhaps more importantly, by discussing these issues and opening up the possibilities for new ways of thinking and believing, you'll help your parents come to terms with their own spirituality. Just the fact of talking about these ideas gets the brain rolling.

It can be fun and revealing to open up the conversation to other family members as well. Most everyone has a slightly different take on spirituality, and some veer widely from common thought. These are fabulous opportunities to expose your parents to new beliefs and possibilities. They'll reject some right off the bat. "Too touchy feely for me!" is a common response to many New Age belief systems.

But other family members will have thoughts similar to theirs, yet different enough to get the mind expanding. If you're lucky, there will be extended family members from various religions. It can be a great holiday meal when you have Jews and Christians and Buddhists all breaking bread around one dinner table.

When you look at your parents' beliefs, you may find an opportunity to gently encourage them to get out there and explore different religions on their own. Maybe suggest they take up meditation or yoga, or check out the local synagogue or mosque or Baptist church. All these places welcome curious, open-minded people. With time, your parents will settle on what comes most comfortably to them. They may find that the most comfortable place is the place where they've always been. The exercise however, will deepen their belief and will assure them that they have a meaningful spiritual home.

Discovery of this sort is a process. It doesn't happen overnight, in fact, many say it takes a lifetime. But there's no better time to get started than now. There's no right way to approach or think about spirituality, just like there's no wrong way either. There's only the way that seems right to you. It'll be different for each of us. What you can do is give your parents the space, encouragement, and support to discover their own.

Fortunately, spiritual options have become more open in the last decades, and it's now common to discuss these issues. Oprah, arguably one of the most widely watched TV personalities of all time, frequently has spiritual topics.

Even the AARP has a "Spirituality and Faith" section on their Web site. This might be an excellent place to get your parents started.

Spirituality in Grief and Illness

Those of us who have lost a loved one to serious illness, or have been diagnosed with one themselves, know how quickly this event leads to deeper, spiritual questioning. In fact, according to an article published by the Hospice Foundation of America, "spirituality and health" is actually a new field in healthcare.[113] The author, Dr. Christina Puchalski, is the executive director of the George Washington Institute for Spirituality and Health in Washington, D.C., and a professor of medicine and health sciences at The George Washington University School of Medicine.

Puchalski writes, "Each person has a story with spirituality being an essential part of the story.... By telling their story, patients can find what gives their lives meaning. This is especially true of people in the midst of suffering, stress, and illness."[114]

According to the National Consensus Conference on Inter-professional Spiritual Care in Palliative Care, Dr. Puchalski defines spirituality as "the aspect of humanity that refers to the way individuals seek and express meaning and purpose and the way they experience their connectedness to the moment, to self, to others, to nature, and to the significant or sacred."[115]

While most clinical settings today are quite impersonal, Dr. Puchalski presents a new set of ideas—and practical tools for achieving these ideas—regarding integrating the value of spiritual beliefs into healthcare. Often it's only when a major illness or other health issue arises that we delve into the murky waters of spirituality. If the illness appears or is diagnosed suddenly, we may be woefully underprepared for the deeper questions that surface. However, we want to discuss them no matter what.

---

113 Dr. Christina Puchalski, *Spirituality and End-of-Life Care*, part of the Living With Grief® series, Hospice Foundation of America, 2011, http://store.hospicefoundation.org/product.php?productid=241

114 *Ibid.*, p. 35

115 Improving the Quality of Spiritual Care as a Dimension of Palliative Care: The Report of the Consensus Conference, http://www.ishtmc.com/sites/default/files/ImprovingTheQulaityOfSpiritualCareInPalliativeCareJPM.pdf

Dr. Puchalski references a study surrounding patients in a family practice setting. Ninety-five percent surveyed wanted their spiritual beliefs addressed in the case of serious illness, 86% if admitted to the hospital, and 60% during a routine history.[116]

Whether we realize it or not, we're a spiritual people who want our most important beliefs voiced and respected.

We saw from previous chapters how a healthy attitude extends our lives. As well, those who are at peace with their spiritual beliefs tend to have better mental health overall and, therefore, live longer. Dr. Puchalski references another study where HIV positive patients who scored high on a spirituality scale had more optimism and a greater will to live.[117]

Another study noted how the majority of patients diagnosed with cancer ranked "faith and belief" as very important to their lives.[118] When we stare our mortality in the face, we ask big questions. This is especially true in the illness and grief setting.

Dr. Puchalski promotes the idea of a new model in healthcare, one where spiritual beliefs are addressed as readily as blood pressure. Here, attending to the patient's needs is the responsibility of every healthcare professional.

This process begins with a spiritual "screening" where the patient's beliefs and vulnerability are noted through a series of questions. "Spiritual distress" could be identified through "despair, hopelessness, abandonment by God or others, isolation from a religious community, inability to forgive, and lack of meaning."[119]

If any of these issues is identified, the clinician would then go about prescribing a treatment. This could range from referral to a therapist to yoga or meditation classes to meeting with the facility's spiritual director for further guidance. Each clinician doesn't have to be an expert in spirituality; they just have to be able to recognize the symptoms of malaise in this area and go about finding the correct avenue to pursue.

---

116 Puchalski, Spirituality and End-of-Life Care, Op. cit., p. 36
117 *Ibid.*, p. 37
118 *Ibid.*, p. 42
119 *Ibid.*, p. 38

Obviously, this isn't at all what the current reality in the healthcare world is like. In fact, both the patient and her doctor might find the whole setting suspect. However, there's huge validity in treating spirituality distress during the time of added stress in illness or grief.

This can be a role that you can play. If you detect the above spiritual distress symptoms, you can talk to your parents. Bring up the issues that concern them most. Ask them how they feel about dying. How afraid are they of pain and illness? Then make suggestions for ways to come to terms with their spirituality in this environment.

Dr. Puchalski claims that just by bringing up the conversation provides enormous relief. The answers aren't nearly as important as the ability to discuss the questions. This is a wonderful opportunity for you to add value in this time of extreme sensitivity. Perhaps one day the medical community will catch on that our mind and bodies are incredibly linked and spirituality has a place in the physical well-being setting.

The Benefits of Finding Peace

So what happens when your parents finally reach a peaceful place with their spirituality? What are their lives going to look like? Will they wear white robes and chant their way through the day? Probably not.

Bob Lowry, a blogger for satisfyingretirement.blogspot.com, described it this way: "There are several benefits that I believe have come from my enhanced spiritual life. One is an overall sense of calm and peace.... Until seven or eight years ago, I was stressed, uptight, looking to blame others, short-tempered, verbally abusive, anxious.... in short, a mess. I was a type A person with a capital A."[120]

Does that sound like anyone you know? Bob said it didn't happen overnight, but through the years, as he paid more attention to his spiritual self and found his priorities shifting. No longer was his work most important. Achieving business goals and making sure every single client walked away satisfied didn't end up being the most important activity to him. Rather, he rediscovered his wife and children, who had patiently waited for him, and

---

120 Bob Lowry, "A Hidden Piece of the Puzzle," October 5, 2011, http://satisfyingretirement.blogspot.com

created a new circle of friends who appealed to the calmer, more introspective Bob.

He claims a large part of the success of his retirement was coming to terms with the big questions involved in spirituality.

Gratitude

Molly Srode is the author of the book *Creating a Spiritual Retirement: A Guide to the Unseen Possibilities in Our Lives.* She describes an experience with gratitude in relation to her refining her spirituality.

"Several years ago, I attended a retreat at which the leader directed us in a unique exercise. He told us to touch our eyes and to thank that part of our body for all those years of faithful service. We thanked our eyes for the years of eyestrain in studying for exams and being subjected to chlorine in swimming pools. We thanked them for the beauty they had brought to us and how our sight had kept us safe on many occasions. We paused for a few minutes and then we went on to the next part of the body. We quietly meditated on how our ears had faithfully served us. By the time we reached our shoulders, tears were streaming down my face.

"How hard I had been on my body all these years, with never an expression of appreciation! For the first time I experienced compassion for my body. In doing so, I experienced compassion for myself."[121]

What Molly is describing is the powerful influence of gratitude. We have so much to be grateful for, even when it seems like the world is crashing down on us. Despite illness, family troubles, or just the annoying fact we keep losing our keys, Molly's experience shows us what we truly have to appreciate. Just take your eyes. Despite the fact they may need a little bit of help nowadays, they've done a fine job for the decades we've been using and abusing them.

With this new mindset, you will realize we have a mighty lot to be grateful for. Bring this thought to the attention of your parents during the talk.

---

[121] Molly Srode, excerpt from *Creating a Spiritual Retirement: A Guide to the Unseen Possibilities in Our Lives*, (Woodstock, VT: SkyLight Paths Publishing, 2003). Also available online at http://www.spiritualityandpractice.com.

It's a great way to remember the good in life and all that's actually working in our favor.

The Boomer Take on Spirituality

Baby boomers have acclimated to different forms of spirituality. Those who spent their teens and twenties in the 60s and 70s, some now self-proclaimed "ex-hippies", were exposed to the breakdown of traditions, actively searched for paths filled with more meaning, and experienced the New Age set of spiritual beliefs. Self-help "gurus" such as Wayne Dyer, Eckhart Tolle, and Deepak Chopra write books that sell in the millions and give widely viewed seminars and talks espousing New Age beliefs. (The term "New Age" is actually a misnomer, as many of these ideas go back centuries, and even millennia, to eastern religious beliefs. For example, feng shui, the art of balancing the energy in your living areas, dates back to at least 1,000 B.C. China.)

Given all this exposure, baby boomers and beyond are more familiar with various spiritual beliefs. From reincarnation to meditation to feng shui, it's simply not as strange as it might have been for your parents. Self-help books by New Age authors are stacked in bookstores right along with the latest romances and thrillers.

So if your parents come from either the "hippie sixties" or the New Age wave, you may have a much easier time discussing spirituality with them and getting them into a place of peace. If they weren't influenced by either of these cultural events, it still means you have a plethora of resources available to you. At the very least, step into your local bookstore (or browse Amazon if you no longer have a local bookstore) and find something that will give them a wide array of beliefs to consider. This is a great way to begin the search for spiritual meaning in their lives.

Remember, inner peace doesn't appear overnight. It's a process, one of personal discovery that no one can do on their own behalf.

Robert Martin Walker, blogging on *Soul In Motion*, described it this way: "Spiritually, [in] retirement can be the most fertile time of life. Free from the pressures of a full-time job, we have more time to enjoy those activities and practices that feed our souls. In Hinduism, this time of life is called the 'forest dweller' stage."[122]

In other words, finding your spiritual base is a wonderful journey, and retirement is an ideal time for it to take place. With the right attitude, your parents can enjoy the discovery process and comes to terms with this aspect of their legacy.

In Summary

Retirement is a time for your parents to pursue their passions. They'll not only be happier, but they'll also actually live longer. I hope that you've learned from this section that it's incredible what a healthy mental state can achieve for us. It's important for each of us to recognize that even in times of stress and loss, life is good.

You can help by guiding your parents in the direction that will give them the most happiness and love. You can educate them on choices that will help transition them successfully to retirement, leave a legacy, gain peace of mind in end-of-life issues, create more love in their lives, and, finally, begin the journey of spiritual peace. After all, you're never too old to search for and find your inner spiritual sanctum.

What a wonderful opportunity you have to show them your love and gratitude. In the next section I'll carry on with helping them find ways to pursue their passion in life and stay actively involved.

---

[122] Robert Martin Walker, "Retirement Redefined," April 15 2010, http://soulinmotion.blogspot.com

Section Five

Staying Involved and the Talk

25

The Secret Ingredient to Longevity

Some of the longest-living and happiest people come from a small island in Greece called Ikaria. This tight-knit community has such a history of longevity that researchers have gathered to unravel their secret.

So far, studies show the people on Ikaria reach the ripe old age of 90 at two-and-a-half times the rate of Americans, with men at four times the rate of their American counterparts. As well, the onset of chronic illness such as heart disease and cancer is delayed in Ikaria by up to ten years, and dementia sets in at only 25% the rate it does here in the States.[123] Not only do these island inhabitants live longer, but they live healthier, too.

Could it just be all that healthy Mediterranean food and fresh Aegean air? Apparently, it's not. On a neighboring island, just over nine miles away, the longevity rate is much lower than on Ikaria, and the onset of chronic illness arrives earlier, much like in America.[124] Something else is at work.

The diet on Ikaria supports longer and healthier living, exactly as I had discussed in Section Three, "Physical Health and the Talk." The basic diet is heavy in fresh vegetables, including wild greens, as well as potatoes and beans, while low in dairy and red meat. Sounds familiar? Goat's milk is used rather than cow's milk, and honey is a common sweetener. In addition, as Dr. Christina Chrysohoou, from the University of Athens School of Medicine, found, people on Ikaris "consumed about six times as many beans a day

---

[123] Dan Buettner, "The Island Where People Forget to Die," *The New York Times,* October 24, 2012
[124] *Ibid.*

as Americans, ate fish twice a week and meat five times a month, drank on average two to three cups of coffee a day, and took in a quarter as much refined sugar—the elderly did not like soda." Dr. Chrysohoou "also discovered they were consuming high levels of olive oil along with two to four glasses of wine a day."[125]

So it's like the low glycemic index (GI) diet, but only more so. The people also sleep late and nap almost every day. However, these factors alone aren't enough to explain the much higher longevity combined with better health on this remote island. The answer appears to be in another category altogether, and this has proven to be true in other pockets of high longevity.

The people on Ikaria have a deeply knit social structure. Although there's an almost 40% rate of unemployment, everyone contributes to his or her community in some way. You're expected to. It's simply the way they live, even if it's just a matter of growing a garden and sharing the proceeds. Almost every evening, people gather and drink wine, relate stories, and relax with people they might have know their entire lives. It's this deep connection with other people that researchers are beginning to believe is the secret ingredient for longevity when combined with a healthy lifestyle. And it's this deep social connection that is the fourth key to your parent's safe retirement.

The Japanese use the word *ikigai* to describe "the reason for which you get out of bed."[126] This is the same idea. When you have a healthy social structure, you have a sense of purpose and belonging. Dan Buettner, who reported on Ikaria for *The New York Times*, wrote that "[a]s soon as you take culture, belonging, purpose or religion out of the picture, the foundation for long healthy lives collapses. The power of such an environment lies in the mutually reinforcing relationships among lots of small nudges and default choices."[127]

From Ikaria to Iowa

Part of the emphasis during the talk should be on making sure your parents

---

125 *Ibid.*
126 *Ibid.*
127 *Ibid.*

don't succumb to loneliness. They need to develop and nurture a satisfying social network. For your parents to truly thrive in retirement, which means not only having more fun but also living longer and healthier lives, they need to build and maintain a web of friends and family. You can play a vital role in this process.

For some, this will be easy. Your parents may be naturally social, and when you explain the health and longevity advantages, they may become even more so. For others, your parents lean toward the hermit side, or perhaps, upon retiring, they seem to have lost their sense of worth and perceived place in society. Here you can step in with not only educating them on the importance of a social network, but also setting the example.

Invite them to family events—dinners, movies, outings with the grandkids. Or if this isn't possible, encourage them to get out there and join clubs or groups or any of the other myriad ways I'll explain on how to become and stay socially active. Sometimes it becomes the adult child's role to play the part of the adult to their parents.

Beware of taking on too much yourself, however. This is a team process, and you're only one player. This is one of the reasons why it's important to have the talk as early as possible. When your curmudgeonly parent realizes that having friends and being involved isn't so bad after all, they'll develop their own momentum in staying busy. It's not all up to you. But you can play that critical role by explaining the issues and developing a plan of action for finding solutions.

Let's look at some of the ways staying involved can be fun and rewarding.

26

Begin at Home

The most logical and heartfelt place to begin staying involved is right at home with family. Again, this doesn't mean you need for your parents to move in with you so they have a strong social network. Instead, the entire family can play a role, including your brothers and/or sisters. If your siblings understand how important staying involved is for their parents, they'll be more motivated to chip in and get involved, too.

Geography doesn't always make this easy, but I will cover solutions to this issue through social media later. The point is for everyone to get involved in getting and keeping your parents involved. Scheduling holiday get-togethers is one such example, whether it's going to church, sitting down for holiday meals, or other family traditions.

Make sure the grandchildren are part of the process. Your parents will love being an active part of their lives. And your children will benefit from closeness to this older and oftentimes mysterious generation.

It's important for you is to be close to your parents, but not too close. They're adults and can work out their lives. Your role is to serve as a guide and help them become aware of issues that will make their retirement years that much better. You can help them avoid pitfalls that many others have fallen right into.

Strengthening Marriage After Retirement

The quality of our parent's marriage can be somewhat of an awkward subject to consider. But how many times have you heard of an outwardly "happy" couple filing for divorce out of the blue? The kids can even get caught off guard because the parents kept their troubles private to all but each other. Perhaps they didn't even know the extent of their marital unhappiness until one, or the other, or both of them are retired.

Studies have shown that the average working couple spends only 20 minutes in conversation a day.[128] Jobs, kids, and outside activities fill up our days, and we're left with very little time for that most important individual in our lives—our spouse. Now consider the ramifications when both parties are thrown together 24/7 upon retirement.

Despite the fact that these people may have been married for decades and even raised a family together, the suddenness of spending so much additional time together can bring up deeper problems that had spent years safely ignored or hidden.

The issue seems to be lessened if the wife retires and the husband continues to work. The domestic roles pretty much remain the same, but the wife now has time to pursue other interests. However, deeper problems can arise when the husband retires and only the wife sets the alarm for each morning. She can end up not only working a full-time job, but also managing the majority of the household chores, all while the husband goes golfing or otherwise does whatever he likes in retirement. Needless to say, this is fertile ground for growing resentment.

Added to this, the husband may be in need of company when she gets home, while all she can think of is having a little space and time to herself. There just isn't enough of her to go around.

When couples retire simultaneously, each person is all of a sudden spending a whole lot of time with someone they may love, but aren't used

---

[128] Marilyn Gardner, "Making Marriage Work After Retirement," *The Christian Science Monitor*, August 30, 2006

to being with as much as they now are. These issues have solutions, but they need to be addressed early on before problems deepen. Retirement, all on its own, is a seismic shift in lifestyle. Add to this the close proximity of a spouse—all the time—and the relationship can be dramatically affected.

Remember, not all relationships suffer upon retirement. Many couples slip happily into a post-retirement routine that suits both sides. However, it's important to be aware of potential trouble spots and how to deal with them early.

Steps to Strengthen

Let's look at seven concrete ways your parents can work toward shoring up any weak spots in their marriage upon retirement.

Communication. Given the astounding statistic that the average working couple only communicates with each other directly for 20 minutes a day, this becomes the logical place to begin strengthening a relationship. Over the years we can take each other for granted. Sending flowers becomes a distant memory, and special dinners or date nights are something you "used to do."

Encourage your parents to take the time to communicate clearly with each other about their retirement goals and dreams. How do they envisage spending each day together? Importantly, how much time do they need *away* from each other every day? Personal space is huge for some people, and when it's invaded regularly, problems arise.

Many happily married couples have different hobbies and activities they passionately pursue, and some even take separate vacations. The point is that each person's needs are met in a respectful and loving way.

Many studies have shown that the way couples speak to each other reveals the quality of the relationship's foundation. Ask your parents to consider this carefully. Are they constantly critical of each other? Do they always bring up the negative side of what the other is doing? Or, do they say supportive and positive things to each other every day? This can be as simple as, "Thank you for emptying the dishwasher." The little stuff builds up, so it's important for every couple to treat their marriage with care and respect.

What happens is we get into habits. The trick is to break the bad ones and nourish the good ones. This very much applies to communicating with our spouse.

Agree Upon Household Chores. Statistically, women still do more of the day-to-day household work than men. The fact that we're living in the 21st century hasn't completely blurred these roles, especially in older generations. Upon retirement, especially if the wife continues to work, this subject needs to be revisited. What your parents end up agreeing to is their business, but encourage them to bring it out in the open and discuss it among themselves.

Quality Time. Encourage your parents to spend quality time together each day. This doesn't mean deciding who makes the salad, but how about an evening walk after dinner? Or doing the crossword puzzle together each morning? Maybe they have a television show they both love and can watch and talk about together. These small actions will help rekindle aspects of the relationship that may have been smothered by years of busy lives.

Mutual Interests. This fits right in line with creating quality time together. If your parents are having trouble reconnecting, suggest they take up a new hobby or activity together. They get the adventure of learning something new, along with the companionship and shared experience of doing it together. Whether it's gourmet cooking classes, learning to play tennis, or taking up Spanish lessons for that dream trip to South America, the potential is there to bring them closer.

Creating Space. Whether or not your parents have been workaholics or just plain addicted to being busy, creating space to pursue their own interests and passions will most probably be important.

Just as creating quality time together through daily habits and new interests is important, equally, each person needs time to be either alone or involved in something without their spouse. Like pillars that stand apart yet support the weight of the roof, strong marriages mean both sides get the space and individual time they need. How your parents decide to handle individual space is their business. Your job is to encourage them to at least talk about it.

Renewing Their Vows. I once met a couple who renewed the wedding vows of their successful marriage every year. Well, almost every year. The one year they didn't, they ended up having a terrible year relationship-wise. Although your parents don't need to go to this extreme, some couples renew their vows upon retirement. This act restates their commitment to each other, and does so in a way that can involve family and friends. It's also a great way to inspire them to take off on a romantic cruise to celebrate their second honeymoon.

Counseling. If your parents seem to be struggling with their relationship during retirement, or anytime for that matter, suggest they seek professional counseling. Many marriages have been saved by a trained third party stepping in and helping the couple frame the issues more objectively. If necessary, remind them that going to a counselor isn't anything to be ashamed of; rather, it's a positive sign that they both want to work to put their relationship back on course.

Relationships Evolve

This is true when dating, during the first years of marriage, while raising the kids, and certainly within the transition to retirement. It is essential that your parents continue to communicate. When issues arise, they should negotiate solutions. In those first weeks, months, and even years of retirement, your parents may find they're not living with the same relationship dynamics they were expecting.

Not only are they spending more time with one individual—their spouse—they may be experiencing the normal challenges that occur upon retirement. For men, this can be a loss of identity that they previously received from their job status. Women can feel the need to take care of everyone, which now includes her husband, and a loss of her own space and normal routine.

Either may be suffering from the gradual physical and mental decline that comes with aging. These extra factors can aggravate any relationship, especially now that they're together all day, every day!

However, with a little planning and thought, a smooth marriage transition into retirement can also be achieved. Your job is to bring the possible problems to the attention of your parents, and then help to show them solutions from which they can choose.

27

Places to Play

As your parents transition to retirement, their day-to-day lives will morph dramatically. No longer is it up at six and at the office by eight, only to return in the evening tired and ready for dinner. Now all that time spent working gets to be filled with whatever they choose.

So where else, other than the family, can your parents go to build this rich, social network that will be so important to their ability to thrive in retirement?

The most logical place for your parents to get involved outside of the family is within the local community. Sometimes the greatest opportunities lie at our front doors.

Getting Started

If your parents were already involved at the community level, such as through local or church-based groups, when they were working, then starting there can be an obvious solution. If they like, they can simply become more involved with that local group or activity. However, if they have not been involved, or if they want to explore new areas of interest, a smorgasbord of choices exists.

The first step is to get your parents on board with the idea of beginning to looking for places and things to be involved in. Sitting around the house all day doesn't lead to happiness. Next, what interests them? Ask but don't fill in the blanks on their behalf; you may be surprised as to what they come up with. I have a friend who took up belly dancing when she retired. It's the last thing I would have expected of her, but she loved it and made a bunch of belly dancing new friends. Now she's joined the local croquet club. Croquet? I didn't even know a club existed!

Discussing ideas for getting involved and continuing growth can be fun in and of itself. Bring it up at dinner with other family members and see how the ideas flow. Make suggestions, by all means, but always stop and listen to what makes their heart pound, not yours.

Clubs are an excellent way for your parents to surround themselves with like-minded people and simultaneously partake in something they love to do. Many clubs have Web sites, so it's just a matter of googling the subject and the location. They can dig up groups that are into mahjong, gourmet cooking, acting, writing—the list goes on endlessly.

One excellent way to be involved and also keep fit is to join an athletic club or group. Let's say they want to take up cycling. Most bicycle repair shops will be in the loop regarding any clubs in the area. Your parents can then start biking on a regular basis and get prepared for that 16-day bike trip in Tuscany they've been dreaming of.

How about golf? Or tennis? Or, as my friend discovered, croquet? All levels of yoga exist; they can begin with one style and move to another.

If your parents live in an assisted living facility or a senior living community, chances are they'll have an array of clubs to choose from, right at their doorstep. A Willow Valley retirement community in Pennsylvania even has a model train club—how unique is that?

Consider also community centers. Here your parents can have access to exercise facilities, clubs, theater groups, painting classes, or tutorial services.

Most churches sponsor activities, classes, and workshops, and if your parents don't have their own regular place of worship, perhaps they can join yours. Here they can mingle with people of their own faith and also discover new areas of interest.

One great part about becoming involved locally is it's easy to nurture the new friendships created. They meet people in person, rather than online, and can expand on these relationships by having dinner parties, barbecues, or other get-togethers away from the activity itself.

Sit down with your parents and understand what interests they'd like to pursue. What will make them happy socially as they continue on this journey called retirement?

City Sites

A great place to find community activities is in the city where they live. I'm amazed at the amount of activities listed on city Web sites for retirees and seniors. For example, the Jersey City Web site has an entire section devoted to adult and senior activities listed under the Department of Recreation.[129] From ballroom dancing to bowling to water aerobics to yoga, their Web site lists where and when.

The town of Jupiter, Florida, has an "Activities for 50+" page. Here they promote seminars on safe driving, monthly dances, how-to classes for the Internet and social media like Facebook and Twitter, and even outings to shopping malls, horse races, and restaurants.[130] It's obviously a bustling place to spend one's free time!

Back to School

Consider also whether or not your parents might like to take classes or even pursue a higher degree at this stage of their lives. Stories abound of those 50 years old and above going back to college to pursue degrees in passions they'd long left dormant. Maybe they had to bypass a dream career to pay the bills or raise a family. Now's the time they can take up the reins again in their education. It's never too late and they're never too old. Be sure and remind them of that.

Or, maybe just a few online classes will do the trick. Perhaps your mom wants to learn to write children's stories while dad wants to finally unravel the secrets of Excel 2010. Check out www.ed2go.com for an easy and plenti-

---

[129] http://www.cityofjerseycity.com/recreation.aspx?id=3886
[130] http://www.jupiter.fl.us/ParksRecreation/SeniorActivities/index.cfm

ful source of courses. Also, many community colleges and universities provide online courses. These can either be taken on their own or with the goal of obtaining a degree.

An inexpensive and convenient way to explore new educational areas is by going to Apple's iTunes Store and searching through iTunes U. Here there are many free classes offered on a myriad of subjects, many from top-notch schools like Stanford or MIT. You may even want to get your parents some DVDs and audio discs of college courses offered by the Teaching Company as a holiday or birthday gift as a way to "nudge" them along.

Often the perfect formula for community activities is a little bit of everything. Maybe your parents will want to join the local bridge club together, but then each pursues independent hobbies (model train building for dad; herb gardening for mom). As the years progress, these may roll over into new pursuits. But for that to happen, they need to stay involved and committed to their social lives. By discussing this topic with your parents and spending some time researching the many opportunities that exist, you'll get them on the road to building that critical social network.

28

Sails Ahoy

Travel is the classic, stereotypical pastime of retirees. Whether driving their RV into the sunset or sipping piña coladas on the deck of a cruise ship, travel and the Golden Years go hand in hand. This may very well be one of the retirement goals of your parents, and there's no reason why it shouldn't be. Traveling to new and exciting places is one of the great rewards of life.

Traveling is also a great way to stay involved in the world and meet new people. It stimulates the imagination and the intellect, and your parents just never know what interesting people they'll sit next to along the way.

Let's look at ways you can help your parents make travel in retirement more practical and fun.

A Penny Saved

The fact is, travel costs money. Unless your parents really do sell the home and live in that RV, they'll be spending more than they would if they just stayed home and tended the garden. Travel expenses need to be anticipated well in advance and included in their annual financial plan.

Therefore, the first step in planning any adventure is to map out a budget. Your parents can set aside a certain amount for travel each year. If they budget $10,000, $30,000, or $100,000 a year for travel, consider how much they'll allow for each trip. This gives them a framework to plan within. Your parents don't want excess fun and tramping about to darken the long-term picture.

Once they've done this, consider the following seven strategies for getting the best bang for their buck:

1) Confess their age, as hard as it may be on the ego. Senior discounts abound, and there's no reason your parents shouldn't be taking advantage of them. Both the AAA and AARP have membership cards that often garner membership and/or senior discounts.

    Hotels, car rentals, airlines, vacation packages, and even cruise lines often have senior discounts, but often you must ask for them. Don't expect them to just be given to your parents. The exact age of "seniorship" will vary, but they generally start at 50.

    Some chain hotels have senior discount programs. At one point Starwood Hotels (think Sheraton, Westin, and W Hotels) offered a whopping 50% discount in their senior program. At Hilton it's 40%. However, be sure and check as discounts may change and so do the programs offered.

2) Ask and ask again. As I said above, most of the time employees aren't going to jump up and ask if you're parents are seniors and want a discount. They need to be proactive. Ask the airlines, the hotels, the B&Bs, and the bicycle rental shop. You never know, and the worst they'll say is "no."

3) Take time planning. When approached with the right attitude, planning the trip is part of the fun. Your parents must take their time and search for the best bargains. As retirees, they have more flexibility around travel dates, so search for the cheapest fares and travel during off-peak seasons.

    Lodging and transportation are the biggest expenses, so consider spending more time in fewer places. For example, your parents can rent an apartment in Buenos Aires, and use that as their base for exploring the rest of the country. Or they can find a central Greek island and book a long-term stay in a B&B. The rates drop dramatically when the B&B knows your parents will be filling that room for a few weeks or months rather than days. Then they'll have more money in their budget to explore the rest of those islands.

4) Go directly to the source. If your parents contact the airline or hotels directly, often they can get a better rate than through a third party, which may take a commission. Remember to ask for senior discounts.

5) Take a tour or cruise. This is a great option, especially for those new to traveling overseas or who simply don't want to be hassled with all the details entailed in organizing a trip. Group tours of a country or region are often cheaper because the organizer gets the advantage of group discounts.

   As well, they'll be taken to places they might not have known about otherwise, and with most, they're educated about the history and local culture as part of the package. They'll also travel with other individuals and couples, which might make the entire trip all the more interesting.

6) Swap their house. Not as crazy as it seems, house swapping with people from all over the world is a popular way to see another country at a reasonable cost. Several reputable Web sites allow travelers to exchange their home with other travelers, which reduces or even eliminates lodging costs altogether. Check out HomeExchange.com and see the amazing array of options available (www.homeexchange.com).

7) Use resources. The AARP Web site, for example, has a plethora of travel ideas and tips (www.aarp.org).

Travel Clubs

Joining a travel club is yet another option. The advantages are much like those of taking a tour. Your parents can partake in organized, cost-effective travel and meet other adventurers along the way; however, the difference is they'll more likely travel with many of the same people and share more experiences with them.

Their community center, church, or Rotary Club may have travel clubs up and running. Also check out national clubs like Road Scholar,[131] Smithso-

---

131   http://www.roadscholar.org

nian Journeys,[132] and Elder Treks.[133] These travel clubs offer comprehensive trips with educated guides who will help your parents get a unique, in-depth experience wherever they go.

With the club option, much of the work is done for you. Your parents get to benefit from other people's experiences and know-how. As well, good ol' group rates will probably apply and they become cost effective, too.

If after doing your research your parents find they have several travel clubs to choose from, consider the following factors to narrow down their search:

- The type of trips. Are they interested in archeological digs or other academic-leaning tours? Or are luxury cruises more their style, with champagne tastings and ballroom dances? How about wilderness hikes or bike tours? Each club will have its own personality, so make sure it fits your parents'.
- Cost range. Check out a few of the trips they've organized and compare the price range to your parents' budget.
- Age and activity. Are your parents going to be traveling with 20-something professionals as they bike 50+ miles a day? (Go for it! Leave 'em in the dust!) Or are walking tours of art museums and theater nights more their style?
- Level of participation. Does one individual or group organize the trips, and your parents just sign up to go along? Or does everyone chip in with ideas and designated jobs?

All these factors add up. With a little due diligence, your parents can find a club that will help them travel well during retirement. It's also motivating to be with other people who also want to travel. Kind of like having walking buddies. You get up on the chilly morning, even though you don't want to, just so you won't let them down. Then you find that was the best walk of all.

---

132   www.smithsonianjourneys.org
133   www.eldertreks.com

Traveling Solo

Unfortunately, many retirees don't have a spouse to travel with. Does this erase travel from the retirement list of dreams? Not a chance. In fact, in a funny way, travel can be better alone. Your parent is forced to get out there and meet people he or she might not otherwise have met. All of the discussed travel tips and ideas apply to individuals as well as to couples.

Consider also group tours and cruises especially tailored to the single- and-senior traveler. Your parent will meet other single travelers and, at the very least, enjoy experiencing some wonderful places in this world with new people. Think of it, right off the bat everyone has something in common—they're all interested in what that cruise or tour has to offer.

If your parent is single and wants a little more oomph to her trip, check out adventure tours for seniors. Just google the phrase and you'll be on your way to finding quality, safe, and active tours for mom or dad. This might just be the type of retirement your parent had in mind.

Remember, just because your parent is alone doesn't mean he or she can't still travel. Given the demographic statistics, more and more single seniors are hitting the road every year. Travel is a great way for them to stay involved and meet amazing new people. Who knows? They might one day bring home that special person who becomes a new step-parent. The world is a wonderful place!

Traveling Safely

Traveling safely is important anytime, but perhaps especially so for a senior who may not be hip to the latest scam or have the cat-like reflexes you used to. We've all heard stories of travel mishaps, which in hindsight could have been prevented or mitigated.

Consider the following list of safety tips to share with your parents during the talk about staying involved and travel:

- Photocopy their passport and driver's license and place these copies in a safe place, other than with the originals. Also, note emergency numbers for credit card companies. This way, should they be robbed, they have the critical information necessary.

- Thoroughly vet the location and safety of the areas they'll be traveling to. Check online travel forums like TripAdviser.com for feedback from other travelers (www. tripadviser.com).
- In this vein, check that their hotel is on a well lit street. They don't want to come home to a strange place in the dark.
- Make sure their suitcases have functioning wheels!
- Check and double-check that they have enough prescription medications for the trip, and include an extra week in case they should be delayed.
- Make sure they have the correct converter plugs for their electrical gadgets, including for their cell phone.
- Keep their carry-on luggage to a minimum or use an airline-approved case with wheels. Security checks and other airport delays can mean long lines, and nothing puts a damper on the experience like back breaking carry-ons.
- If they're flying, make sure they drink lots of water and walk up and down the aisle every couple of hours. This helps prevent blood clots in their legs and generally stretches out stiff bones.
- If they're leaving their hotel room for just a few hours, put the "Do Not Disturb" sign out. This makes people think they're still in the room.
- Place any valuables, including their passport, in the hotel safe.
- Don't wear expensive-looking jewelry. Even if it's fake, it may be enough to attract tourist-hunting thieves.
- Your parents should look at their map before they leave their hotel. They'll probably still have to pull it out on the street, but the less they can do this and mark themselves as obvious tourists, the better.
- Carry a flashlight. Be prepared because they just never know.

- Be careful when taking out money. Place smaller bills in the most commonly used wallet or pocket. Leave the larger stuff for the money belt and open this only when prying eyes are at a minimum. A bathroom makes a great place for reorganizing.

Remember, odds are your parents will have a wonderful, safe trip when planned properly. The above are common sense guidelines to reduce the chance of mishap. It pays to be prudent, especially when they're on someone else's turf.

Learning the Language

Finally, a great combination of staying involved through traveling and stimulating the intellect is to study the language of the country while you're there. It's truly amazing how much more of the local culture and people one can learn just through their language. Your parents will also meet other students and teachers who can help enrich their traveling experience.

The larger the city they're traveling to, the more language learning options they'll have while there. As we do in the 21st century when we want to know about so many things, google it. I typed in "learn Russian in St. Petersburg" and came up with 1.7 million results. The first page alone would keep me happily busy researching both quality and location.

Be sure your parents go to traveling forums to see what other travelers have experienced with the schools or groups they're considering. Then, don't sign up for an enormous and expensive package until they actually get there and have taken a few classes. A beautiful Web site is one thing, but a dingy classroom with a distracted and questionable teacher is another. Although this won't likely happen, it's prudent to sample the goods before they buy them. Have a Plan B and C ready to go if upon arrival their first choice isn't what they expected (maybe a Rosetta Stone language course purchase at the airport may be just the thing).

Many travelers use the combination of an extended stay in one location with learning the local language to form a deep and unique experience with that country and people. This is different from stumbling through in a jet-lagged haze. Your parents will be making a commitment to that trip that could very well change their lives forever. It's not for everyone, but give your parents the options and see how they respond. It may be just the ticket.

29

Getting the Most Out of Working in Retirement

Based on the financial planning work you and your parents did in Section Two, they may need to work part-time during retirement. However, interestingly, finances aren't the only reason retirees look for a paycheck. Many people just want to keep on staying involved. They're ready to "retire," but not to stop being actively working.

A survey conducted by the Employee Benefit Research Institute found that in 2011, 74% of Americans said they would continue to work at least part-time during retirement.[134] For many people this is because they simply don't have enough money. Maybe they didn't save enough along the way or the rising cost of healthcare has them cornered or maybe the economic downturn took a big bite out of their 401(k) plan. But other people work because they want to, pure and simple.

Whatever the reason, working during retirement doesn't have to be a terrible ordeal. In fact, this is a time to realize dreams. They can just be dreams of a different sort: the paying kind. I've spoken to many pre-retirees who claim they'll never stop working. For them it's the purpose that changes. After a certain point, they're not working for the paycheck, although they enjoy receiving it; they're working because they know they're making a difference.

During both the "Financial" and the "Staying Involved" talks, it's vital to discuss the subject of work and how it will impact your parent's finances and

---

134 "Are You Considering Working During Retirement?" Employee Benefit Research Institute, http://www.Prudential.com

quality of life. The idea being that if they're going to work, maybe they want to stay in the same industry as they were before. Or maybe they want to try something completely new.

For example, I have a friend who was the CFO for a division of a Fortune 500 company. She is bright, savvy, and had managed to negotiate her way through the dog-eat-dog world of corporate hierarchy. There was no way she wanted anything to do with that when she retired. Instead, she works part-time at the local garden nursery. Plants are her passion, and she's learning and staying involved in something she absolutely loves. You can suggest the same kind of seismic change for your parents.

I have another friend who ran an overseas division of a different corporate behemoth. He, on the other hand, did want to stay involved because he loved seeing the projects he founded continue to grow and branch into new endeavors. But he didn't want to work full-time. Now he's a consultant for the firm, working a whopping 50 days a year, four weeks of which are traveling to Japan for his business. Not a bad solution either.

Each situation is different, but it's important to understand that your parents don't have to stay in the same ol' job, unless they want to. If they plan on working during retirement, present them with options. Explain that maybe there's a different passion they want to pursue. When done this way, working during retirement can be a wonderful, positive experience. They'll grow with the new role and meet new people who share similar interests.

One excellent option is to suggest they work somewhere where there are younger people. Green hair and pierced noses aside, there's nothing like the young to make you feel and act young yourself. Making vanilla lattes at Starbucks? Why not? They'd make extra income, meet lots of people, have a startling array of colleagues, and learn how to steam up a mean cappuccino.

Let's start by dispelling some myths and examine some realities about working during retirement.

Social Security Benefits and Working Before Full Retirement Age

You've heard it before and maybe have said it yourself, "I can't work during retirement because I'd lose my Social Security benefits." Let's have a closer look at the facts and the fiction in this statement.

First of all, you'll never "lose money" by working in retirement. The end result is you'll make more, period. You may have to pay taxes, yes, but you'll still end up making money. The confusion surrounds how extra income effects Social Security payments.

Currently, full retirement age as determined by the Social Security Administration (SSA) is 66 years old if you were born between the years of 1943-1954. It's somewhat younger if you were born earlier, and gradually extends out if you were born later. If you were born in 1960 or later, your full retirement age is 67.

However, you can begin receiving your Social Security benefits at 62 (I discuss the pros and cons of doing this in my *Safe 4 Retirement* book; furthermore, I find that financial advisors can help with this decision as well). The concern comes if you elect to take early Social Security payments, yet also continue to work specifically during those years between age 62 and 66 or 67 (depending on what your full retirement age is).

In 2012, if you were not of full retirement age but were collecting payments, then they deducted $1 from your benefits for each $2 earned above $14,640. That number will change so visit the Social Security Web site for the latest numbers.[135] However, that money is not lost forever, and this is where the confusion comes in. Rather, that benefit you did not receive will instead be paid out when you reach full retirement age.

In the surprisingly clear words of the government itself, "You can get Social Security retirement or survivors benefits and work at the same time. But, if you are younger than full retirement age and earn more than certain amounts, your benefits will be reduced. It is important to note, though, that

---

[135] http://www.ssa.gov

these benefit reductions are not truly lost. Your benefit will be increased at your full retirement age to account for benefits withheld due to earlier earnings."[136]

So that's good news. Yes, your benefits are reduced while you're working before your full retirement age. But, no, those benefits are not lost forever, as you will actually get them back in just a few short years.

The SSA's Web site is actually a great resource for questions of this type. Believe it or not, it's clearly written and answers most everything you can think of asking in this realm.

Social Security Benefits and Working After Full Retirement Age

This is another area of confusion. Yes, you can work after your full retirement age and still receive your Social Security benefits. This time, however, those benefits will be taxed after a certain level, and, for some reason, they like to make this a little complex. (If you don't work during retirement, those benefits are not taxable.)

When you file your taxes, Form 1040A will walk you through the calculations for determining the taxability of your benefits. The SSA provides the following "quick computation":

- Take the entire amount of income you made during the year, including tax-exempt interest and other exclusions from taxable income.
- Add half the amount of your Social Security benefits for that year.
- Compare that total with the base amounts for the year you're in.

For example, in 2010, any benefits received over the following base amount—per the formula above—were taxable:

- $32,000 for married couples filing jointly.
- $25,000 for single, head of household, qualifying widow/widower with a dependent child, or married individuals filing separately who did not live together during the year.

---

136 http://www.ssa.gov/pubs/10069.html

Remember that you're not losing money; you're simply being taxed on your benefits. You're still making more money than if you didn't work at all. Your job during this part of the talk is to make sure your parents are absolutely clear about this, because, for some reason, this is an area rife with misinformation. Don't let these misconceptions send them back to the couch or keeping them away from building social networks outside of their house.

Working Part-Time

So hopefully, we've cleared the air a bit about the monetary reality of working during retirement. Now let's consider another option your parents have: working part-time. Both of the cases I described previously were regarding retirees taking on part-time work. Yet, how can you "be retired" and yet be working full-time?

First of all, downscaling to working part-time can be a great way to retire early. After all, they're still bringing in an income, although less, and they've freed up half their time to begin their new lifestyle. Chances are they'll move into a lower tax bracket, and they can work in the same field or an altogether different one. Within the financial parameters set during the financial review, your parents can make the choices that work for them.

Sometimes people work part-time to cover medical insurance premiums until they hit 65 and qualify for Medicare. Although as we saw earlier, medical expenses certainly don't stop at this point, they're just reduced.

Whatever the reason, ask your parents to search their dreams when they consider working part-time. What type of work would give them the most satisfaction and, yet, be realistic and bring in the amount of income they need, if any? Answering this is important if they are to really enjoy themselves and grow while working during retirement, rather than just tolerating the process. It can open the gateway to new adventures, people, and experiences. It can be an exciting time for your parents and interesting to see how they handle these experiences.

Finding Work as a Senior

So where can your parents go to find work during retirement? We've all heard of cases where people found it difficult to get a job because they were too old. I mean, after all, who wants to hire someone who has a lifetime of experience and wisdom? That doesn't seem to be valued in the business world these days.

In all reality, however, jobs abound for retirees. It's just a matter of knowing where to look and being flexible. As I mentioned before, the first step for your parents is to stop and have a close examination of their heart and dreams. What would they actually love to do? What are they qualified to do? And where do these two meet?

If they know what they want to do and where, they can begin looking. Although this makes the process much simpler, the reality may be that jobs won't always be available in these chosen areas, so they should also be prepared to consider other options as well.

Your parents can get a fast start on their job hunt by considering the following as places to begin their search:

- Current contacts. Who do you or your parents know who can recommend them for a position?
- The local paper and other community publications. Don't forget to check online.
- Churches and community centers. These places often have bulletin boards where jobs and volunteer work are posted.
- Craigslist, Monster.com, and other online job postings. You can tailor the searches geographically and cruise through the choices at your leisure. As with anything online, don't pass on any personal information such as Social Security numbers without knowing for sure whom you're dealing with.

Another successful option is to check out community senior service facilities. Often these can be found online. For example, the Philadelphia Corporation for Aging has a job search facility right on their main Web site.[137] Many cities have services similar to this one.

As well, check out national groups like RetiredBrains.com. Here you can search for jobs, get advice on starting your own small business, and even post positions to hire people yourself.[138] The AARP Web site has career advice and articles on how to find work for those over 50.

They may want to also consider hiring a career counselor. These people are trained to not only help them understand what job will suit them best at this point in their lives, but also help them find the job itself. This can be an efficient alternative especially if they're looking for work that requires specific qualifications.

In all, working during retirement can be a rewarding journey. It needs to be approached the right way, including having a flexible mind and attitude. Your job is to help your parents understand the alternatives so they head in the most positive direction possible.

---

[137] http://www.pcacares.org/ServiceSearchResults.aspx?tab=0&miles=0&serviceType=Employment/Jobs
[138] http://retirementjobs.retiredbrains.com/c/search_results.cfm?site_id=9182

30

Volunteering

In the United States, in 2010 alone, over 62 million adults volunteered over 8 *billion* hours of service. The monetary value of their time and energy is estimated at almost $173 billion.[139] Yet volunteering means that you work for free.

Well, ask any volunteer and they'll tell you they receive far more from volunteering than a dollar amount would show. Ken Charvoz, a retired police officer and volunteer with OASIS in Tucson, Arizona, said, "[Volunteering] gives us a reason to get up and going. It's our paycheck."[140] And evidence shows that volunteering doesn't just make us feel better, it helps us live longer, too.

The Corporation for National and Community Service issued a report entitled, *The Health Benefits of Volunteering*. According to this report, "Over the past two decades, a growing body of research indicates that volunteering provides not just social benefits, but individual health benefits as well. This research has established a strong relationship between volunteering and health: those who volunteer have lower mortality rates, greater functional ability, and lower rates of depression later in life than those who do not volunteer."[141]

It all makes sense when you step back and think about it. For many of us, some of the most memorable experiences of our lives were when someone

---

139   http://www.volunteeringinamerica.gov
140   Dr. Erwin Tan, "The Win-Win of Senior Volunteering," http://www.whitehouse.gov, July 15, 2011
141   *The Health Benefits of Volunteering: A Review of Recent Research*, The Corporation for National and Community Service, http://www.nationalservice.gov/about/volunteering/benefits.asp

came out of the blue and helped us (just in the nick of time?), or when we did the same for them. It just feels right and we all know it.

In this vein, volunteering is one of the most common retirement activities of all. And it's an ideal way to stay involved because not only are we helping people, animals, or our community in some way, but we're meeting new people, too.

When you have the "staying involved" talk with your parents, remind them that volunteering is one way to leave behind a marvelous legacy. With just a few hours a week, they can expand their footprint within their community exponentially.

How do you measure the effect you have on an at-risk child's life when you set a positive example? Or the relief you give an older person who has trouble with basic tasks such as shopping for groceries? What about placing orphaned animals in loving homes rather than them relegated to kill shelters?

To find meaning in their lives, and to *make* more meaning, make sure your parents understand the big picture when it comes to volunteering.

Senior Corps

Senior Corps is an independent federal agency that helps connect people 55 years old and older to community projects and organizations. In their words, "Conceived during John F. Kennedy's presidency, Senior Corps currently links more than 500,000 Americans to service opportunities. Their contributions of skills, knowledge, and experience make a real difference to individuals, nonprofits, and faith-based and other community organizations throughout the United States."[142]

For our purposes in this section, Senior Corps is a great avenue to get your parents involved volunteering in their community. Senior Corps has three main programs they run:

The *Foster Grandparent Program*. Here, volunteers are placed in mentoring roles with children and young adults with exceptional needs. This is

---

142 http://www.seniorcorps.gov/about/sc/index.asp

a phenomenal opportunity to make a positive difference in those lives that need the most help.

The *Senior Companion Program*. Volunteers are placed in companion roles with adults in their community who have trouble performing day-to-day tasks. Companions help by taking the time to stop by and chat, or do simple shopping or chores, or even to interact with doctors. In these cases your parents would be lightening the load for older or disabled individuals.

RSVP. Finally, the RSVP program connects volunteers with service opportunities in their own communities. They base their recommendations on the volunteer's experience and availability. The range is pretty impressive, "[f]rom building houses to immunizing children, from enhancing the capacity of non-profit organizations to improving and protecting the environment,..."[143]

Their Web site makes it easy to find volunteer opportunities in your local area. For instance, when I typed in a zip code for Los Angeles, California, and allowed for a 20-mile search radius, over 1,000 results came in for volunteering.

The RSVP program has local branches throughout the United States. For example, the Shawnee and Douglas Counties of Kansas have an RSVP site that streamlines the process. You simply click on an "Apply to be a Volunteer" button, then state how many hours you have available.[144] It couldn't be easier!

King County in Seattle, Washington, has the same type of easy access through the Solid Ground Web site.[145] Check out your own community for RSVP and Senior Corp volunteer openings. They may very well have something meaningful and convenient your parents would benefit from.

Other Avenues

The opportunities for volunteering are endless. If you or your parents know of a cause or organization that's already of interest, like Habitat for Humanity or the Humane Society, then go right ahead and give them a call. Church-

---

143 *Ibid.*
144 http://www.unitedwaytopeka.org/volunteer/rsvp
145 http://www.solid-ground.org/GETINVOLVED/VOLUNTEER/RSVP/Pages/default.aspx

es and community centers, local schools, and theater and arts groups will almost always have need for volunteers.

Start with what your parents are interested in and begin searching from there. It can be as easy as googling "volunteer opportunities" and the name of your town. For example, the Philadelphia Corporation for Aging, which I mentioned earlier, also has a volunteer section on its Web site.[146] It lists over 140 different opportunities alone. Sometimes one source will lead to several others, the positions branching out like limbs on trees.

When you have the talk about staying involved, make sure you bring up these types of choices. When the right match is made, everyone's lives improve.

Volunteering Overseas

Yes, this is a viable and often life changing opportunity—with a good dose of adventure thrown in. Sometimes we forget that people need help not only here at home, but also throughout the world. The neat thing about this is not only would your parents reap the normal benefits from volunteering, but they'll also get steeped within a foreign culture. Imagine the interesting people they'll meet along the way.

One way to get started volunteering overseas is to utilize travel groups that organize volunteer/travel tours. This way your parents have experienced travelers organizing their trip, and they can sample the volunteering aspect to see if it suits them. It's like taking a vacation to a country, with volunteering thrown in. One such group is Hand Up Holidays, which creates "Meaningful Adventures for the Young at Heart."[147]

Angela Pakes, at the age of 60, traveled to Cambodia and had this to say, "The idea of a 'taste of volunteering' suited me perfectly as a way to find out if volunteering was for me. The holiday was superb and I received a fascinating insight into the country, people, and culture.

"Both the guides and drivers looked after me very well. The hotel accommodation was excellent. My volunteer work was very enjoyable and I believe

---

146 http://www.pcacares.org/Organization_List.aspx?organizationType=Senior%20Center&tab=2&miles=0
147 http://www.handsupholidays.com/read/seniors

it helped, although I felt that I learned more from the students at the school than they did from me."[148]

Isn't that so often the case, that the volunteers learn at least as much, if not more, than the people they're there to help? On the Hands Up Holidays Web site you can do a search for the country, region, and type of volunteering you're interested in.

Another resource is from Transitions Abroad. This group organizes volunteering travel packages, as well as work or study abroad opportunities.[149] These programs are tailored for seniors, and choices exist for which type of volunteering your parents might be interested in. Whether it's teaching reading in a developing nation to restoring historical sites to working with nature and the environment, the choices are astounding.

Yet another resource is the World Volunteer Web Web site. They have an entire section on seniors volunteering and what opportunities are available.[150]

Considerations When Volunteering Overseas

As with all travel and tours, and most any adventure you partake in, do your due diligence. Check out what other volunteers have to say about the quality of organization they experienced. Were they on time and professional? Were the living facilities or hotels clean and in safe locations? Was the volunteer work meaningful and well organized? Apply all the travel safety tips I wrote about earlier.

However, volunteering abroad has a few additional considerations to keep in mind:

- Will the work be physically taxing? Will your parents need to climb hills, walk between villages, or fend off a troop of baboons?
- Are your parents' skills in line with the volunteer work? If they've

---

148 *Ibid.*
149 http://www.transitionsabroad.com/listings/travel/senior/volunteer_vacations_for_adults_and_seniors.shtml
150 http://www.worldvolunteerweb.org/browse/volunteering-issues/senior-volunteers.html

been raising a family for the last 30 years, is hammering nails to build a school what they want to do? If your parent is a retired CPA, is wiring that same school for electricity in his skill set? Maybe so, but still check into the details of the actual work.

- What type of medical care is available? How does the group organize any medical care or emergencies?

- Do your parents have any physical disabilities that would hinder their participation? Developing countries won't have the ease of access and services we do. Consider even things like allergies, claustrophobia, or an extreme fear of spiders or heights.

- Is there someone they can talk to who's taken the tour before? This is an excellent way to get a firsthand account of what to expect.

- Are there Internet connections or some other way to keep in touch with your family while they're away? Your parents may be having the time of their lives while your family is tearing their nails out in worry.

It really boils down to common sense. Your parents should treat their volunteer adventure as they would any other overseas trip, with the added element of helping the community they're visiting.

When it comes to staying involved, volunteering is one of the most satisfying avenues. Yes, they will meet new people who are volunteers and recipients of their goodwill. But your parents will also get the knowledge and peace of mind that they're making a difference in this world. Life isn't over when you retire. Rather, for many, it's when life really starts to make sense.

31

The Magic of Social Media

Remember the Greek island of Ikaria I mentioned at the beginning of this section? Researchers are coming to the conclusion that part of their longevity is due to the tight social structure they live within. However, most of us don't have access to that lifestyle. We live in communities, sure, but we don't have the density of contact the Ikarians have. Add to this the extremely mobile lifestyle that's becoming the norm in America, and many seniors find themselves far away from their families. Their social net becomes thinner as they age, not stronger.

The problem is that the importance of staying connected hasn't been reduced, although our culture often makes it more difficult to do so. We can see this especially with many seniors who end up spending a lot of time alone or may have difficulty getting out of the house to do much. Yet, for them, being part of a community is critical. Depression can easily slip into their worlds when they don't have enough human contact.

Social media can fill this gap, and it isn't that hard to learn. It can give your parents the ability to get together with friends and family, without ever leaving the house.

According to a recent study by the Pew Research Center's Internet & American Life Project, the 74+ demographic is the fastest growing among social networks. *Seventy-four-plus!* Half of adults 65 and older are online, and social networking among this group jumped 100 percent between April 2009 and May 2010. Social networking has almost doubled amongst the 50 and older population, too, with 42% participating.[151] There are even people over the age of 100 who are taking up Facebook![152]

Something interesting is happening with social media and seniors. If your parents aren't online and facebooking yet, it's time to get them there. And it's not just because it's fun.

Dr. Shelia Cotten, a sociologist and Associate Professor at the University of Alabama, conducted a study that found that regular Internet usage was responsible for a 30% decrease in depression in older adults.[153]

In short, social media is a huge opportunity for strengthening the social network that so clearly improves lives physically and mentally. It's bridging the ravine between our mobile work culture and the deep need we have to be socially connected.

Getting Up and Running

Your parents may already be computer savvy. If that's the case, it's just a matter of showing them the benefits of social media. However, for that large group of seniors that still isn't online, the process doesn't have to be difficult. In fact, social media has made the idea of learning how to use a computer less daunting. When they have a clear use for technology, it becomes easier to learn how.

Fortunately, many senior centers, community centers, and assisted living facilities now have classes on computers, the Internet, how to use Facebook, and even sessions called "What's in a Tweet." These are ideal places to learn. The instruction is geared generationally (as opposed to for a 15-year-old whippersnapper who's never even listened to music on a radio), so your parents will be surrounded by other seniors taking the social media plunge.

They can begin with the basics, and then gradually move up to more advanced classes specialized to their interests. Photoshop and Office 2010 are other hot topics. It's the easiest way to keep up with their families.

---

151   Aylin Zafar, "Facebook for Centenarians: Senior Citizens Learn Social Media," The Atlantic, August 31, 2011. Also available online at http://www.theatlantic.com/technology/archive/2011/08/facebook-for-centenarians-senior-citizens-learn-social-media/244357/
152   Ghinwa Yatim, "100-year-old Lebanese grandma a devoted social media user", Al Arabiya News, http://www.alarabiya.net/articles/2012/09/25/240157.html
153   *Ibid.*

Many community colleges have great classes for getting started with computer basics and social media. Online courses also exist, such as those on Education to Go.[154]

Bridging the Generational Divide

The AARP and Microsoft Corporation published a research report entitled, *Connecting Generations*.[155] They wanted to understand how people from different generations were using the Internet and social media.

Two of their main findings were:

- Of those between 13 and 75, 83% said going online was a "helpful" way to communicate with family members. Teenagers, specifically, said going online helped the quantity (70%) and quality (67%) of communicating with family members who lived far away.

- The number of young adults and grandparents are about equal (29% and 30%, respectively) that say communicating with their older/younger relations online has helped them better understand each other.[156]

In a nutshell, when your parents become social media savvy, their world expands. They're in touch with their families more, including those precious grandchildren who grow up far too quickly, as well as with their friends. Once they get the hang of surfing the Web, they can expand on all kinds of interests.

Sandra, who works with the Visiting Nurse Service of New York, said, "It helps people build support systems, make friends, reacquaint themselves with old friends, connect with family, and connect over shared interests, whether that's religion, politics, cooking, health, or anything else. It's an inexpensive way to allow people to stay connected, especially for those for whom mobility, transportation and companionship are hard to coordinate."[157]

---

154 http://www.ed2go.com
155 "AARP and Microsoft Release New Study on How Online Communication Connects Generations," February 7, 2012, http://www.aarp.org/about-aarp/press-center/info-02-2012/AARP-and-Microsoft-Release-New-Study-Communication-Connects-Generations.html
156 Ibid.
157 Ibid.

The Seniors for Living Web site has a list of the top 100 blogs and Web sites for seniors and boomers. Check these out for ideas, information, and support. You'll be amazed at what you find.[158]

Social Media Safety

Just as your parents can reconnect with family and friends online, they can also connect with the seedy underbelly of humanity. Those of us who are more experienced with social media and the Web in general may be more aware and savvy about online scams, but your parents may not. As well, there's also online etiquette to be aware of. You want to gently point your parents in the right direction here, too.

Take a look at the following guidelines:

- Understand privacy options and settings. Teach your parents how to use them. Err on more privacy rather than less.

- Be extra-careful downloading attachments or anything off the Web. Have your parents ask you first until they get a feel for what's legit and what's not.

- Never send personal information like bank account or Social Security numbers online. Phishing is the act of appearing to be a legitimate organization, but in reality they're crooks looking for easy money.

- Don't mention in public posts that you're home alone. You never know who will be interested.

- Ask your teen family members before you "friend" them. They may not feel comfortable letting you see all their posts, so just quietly check that it's okay first.

- Be careful what you post about family members and friends. It may be cute and funny, but what if a potential employer is checking out your niece's Facebook page for her first big job application?

Most of those guidelines are common sense. Chances are that in no time at all, your parents will be up and running their social media lives. Just be sure and check in on what they're doing from time to time, especially at the

---

[158] www.seniorsforliving.com/content/article/top-100-senior-blogs-web-sites/32/

beginning. Scammers target older people because they know they aren't as experienced. But give your parents some time and they will be. Who knows? They might even teach you a few social media tricks before long.

In Summary

I can't emphasize enough the importance of your parents staying involved. It's the social fabric of their lives that provides the main ingredient to longevity. The thicker and more secure this is, the better quality and quantity of their lives. As well, it's just plain more fun. That's a hard one to argue against.

During your "staying involved" talk, point out the benefits of being social, and also just how easy it all is. If they follow the ideas and guidelines I set out in this section, they'll have a retirement rich in new experiences and people. And, at the end of that day, that's what it's all about!

Peace of Mind

When you write a book like this, you struggle with questions such as, "Who is the target market for it?" "In what section of the bookstore will it be found?"

I think that this book will have many people saying similar things that I heard about *Safe 4 Retirement: The Four Keys to a Safe Retirement*. Things like "I enjoyed the book and I think that my children would enjoy it as a way to prepare for retirement" or "The book is best for my retired parents who need to consider all of these many aspects of their lifestyle."

Although my book refers to "the talk" that needs to occur between adult children and their parents, the title assumes that the adult children initiate this talk. Yet, will they always be the ones to do that?

Experience and research has shown that we are seeing more and more parents initiating the talk than ever before. One of my dear friends told me how her parents ended a wonderful family Thanksgiving dinner with the *need* to clarify what their plans were for the rest of their life and beyond. Although this may have brought on indigestion for much of the family, they all agreed (the next day) that having this talk was needed and was the highlight of the holiday. They thanked their mom and dad for having the courage to bring it up.

If you've read this far, I think that you'll now agree with me that that the talk does need to happen, regardless of who brings it up and starts the conversation. Clearly, this is something that most adult children and their parents believe as well.

According to Fidelity's first ever "Intra-Family Generational Finance Study," 89% of families agree that health and eldercare discussions are important. The study goes on to further say that "while more than nine in 10 (94 percent) adult children and their parents agree it is important to have frank conversations about wills and estate planning, eldercare or covering retirement expenses, there are significant barriers to even starting these discussions within families."[159]

Yes, we know that barriers exist. Perhaps having the talk at the Thanksgiving table will not be the best time for most families to do it, but sometimes we just need to seize the moment and just do it.

I hope that I've provided you with some skills and resources to have the talk. Perhaps you'll use some of the conversation starters I gave you or utilize your own stories.

Maybe you'll just jump into it on your own, and all that this book provided you is the motivation to have that conversation.

Does it really matter if you're an adult child or if you're a retiring or retired parent who begins the process?

In this book, I've provided you a road map to follow and, hopefully, have given you the courage and tools you need to have the talk. I've also advocated that the best time to have it is sooner rather than later. I ask you to aim for the talk to occur at the time of a parent's upcoming or early stages of retirement.

The Fidelity study agrees with me on this point: "Parents are more likely to cite when they near or enter retirement (37 percent) as the right time, while children indicate that they'd like to have a conversation before their parents retire or have health issues (37 percent)." The study further points out that "sixty-five percent of adult children and parents agree that discussing retirement readiness is an important topic."

---

159 www.fidelity.com/inside-fidelity/individual-investing/intra-family-generational-finance-study

As with my previous book, I struggled with this book being viewed as strictly a book about retirement. Most books about retirement reside in the personal finance sections of bookstores. At this point, do you feel that this book is strictly, or even primarily, about one's finances?

Many will feel that this book has more to do with personal health or personal growth than personal finance. I've been told that this is more appropriate in the self-help section.

So, now that you've read this book, I ask you, who is this book really for? What category should this book be in?

Surely, the adult children can be the drivers of the talk. As we've seen in this book, the need and the rewards are there for them to go through this process and set up a plan and road map to follow that satisfies the desires of their parents.

Doing this can create a longer and more fulfilling life for their parents, and the rewards for that will reach across the multiple generations of a family. The rewards for doing this will not just be financial, but will also be realized in the smiles and joys found on the faces of parents, children, and grandchildren.

What about those families where the parents recognize this as well, but the reality is that they, not their adult children, will need to be the ones to initiate this process?

The tools and resources are here in this book to allow the parent to initiate the talk with their children.

The important point is that adult children and their parents realize that the talk needs to happen!

The wonderful thing about all of this is that once you have the talk, there is a huge weight off the adult children's and the parents' shoulders, regardless of who initiated it. Anne Tergesen of Marketwatch.com pointed out in an article that refers to the Fidelity Study that "not surprisingly, those who take the time to have these conversations tend to feel better. Fidelity said that 90% of the parents who have had such discussions with their adult children reported having "peace of mind." Only 61% of parents who have not had this talk felt the same way."

So, having the talk will help you achieve "peace of mind"—maybe this really is a self-help book after all!

It doesn't really matter whether you're an adult child or a parent and you've found this book in either the retirement or self-help section, the point is you are holding this book (or Kindle or whatever electronic device you use) and planning the next steps that will lead to having the talk.

My sincere hope is that I've learned from the lame advice that I gave to my parents to *"not collect things,"* and have provided you with a collection of thoughts, ideas, conversation starters, stories, and advice that will allow you, whatever your age, to properly take the next step.

The next step is to do something that I wish I'd had the chance to do with my parents—have the talk!

It starts with love.

About the Author

Jack Tatar is the author of two books that are changing how people view retirement: *Safe 4 Retirement: The Four Keys to a Safe Retirement* and *The 10 Joys of a Safe Retirement*. Jack is CEO of GEM Research Solutions, a leading worldwide market research firm. Jack is a highly sought speaker on many topics and provides regular contributions on retirement to various media outlets including Marketwatch.com and his own site at Safe4Retirement.com.

Jack lives in Pennington, New Jersey with his wife, Maude and his two children.

He can be reached through email at:
Jack@Safe4Retirement.com
or on Twitter
@Safe4Retirement
and on Facebook at
Facebook.com/Safe4Retirement